MINDSET MATTERS

Published by SuccessBooks®, Lake Mary, FL.

SuccessBooks® is a registered trademark.

ISBN: 979-8-9892734-5-4
LCCN: 2024910898

This publication is designed to provide accurate and authoritative information with regard to the subject matter covered. It is sold with the understanding that the publisher is not engaged in rendering legal, accounting, or other professional advice. If legal advice or other expert assistance is required, the services of a competent professional should be sought. The opinions expressed by the authors in this book are not endorsed by SuccessBooks® and are the sole responsibility of the author rendering the opinion.

Scripture quotation marked HCSB is taken from the Holman Christian Standard Bible®, Copyright © 1999, 2000, 2002, 2003, 2009 by Holman Bible Publishers. Used by permission. Holman Chris-tian Standard Bible®, Holman CSB®, and HCSB® are federally registered trademarks of Holman Bible Publishers.

Scripture quotation marked NRSVUE is from the New Revised Standard Version, Updated Edition. Copyright © 2021 by the National Council of Churches of Christ in the United States of America. Used by permission. All rights reserved worldwide.

Most SuccessBooks® titles are available at special quantity discounts for bulk purchases for sales promotions, premiums, fundraising, and educational use. Special versions or book excerpts can also be created to fit specific needs.

For more information, please write:

SuccessBooks®
3415 W. Lake Mary Blvd. #950370
Lake Mary, FL 32746
or call 1.877.261.4930

Visit us online at www.CelebrityPressPublishing.com.

MINDSET
MATTERS

SUCCESS
BOOKS®
Lake Mary, FL

CONTENTS

CHAPTER 1

YOUR MINDSET DETERMINES YOUR SUCCESS

By Jack Canfield

Mindset. It matters. So why do the vast majority of people go through life never understanding the pivotal role that mental attitude—including our thoughts, goals, habits, and behaviors—plays in shaping our journeys and unlocking doors to unparalleled success?

I've discovered that mindset is everything. In fact, there's a specific formula that can help you achieve the success-oriented mindset you need to create the life you want. Let's start with the first part of this equation.

DECIDE WHAT SUCCESS MEANS TO YOU

Have you ever wondered why most people (perhaps you) don't get the results they want? It's because they haven't decided what those *results* are. They haven't defined the lifestyle, income, relationships, experiences, and other outcomes they want—in clear and compelling detail.

After all, how else can your mind know where to begin acting upon your vision if you don't give it specific and detailed results to achieve?

> The indispensable first step to getting the things you want out of life is this: decide what you want.
>
> —BEN STEIN
> WRITER, ACTOR, AND SOCIAL COMMENTATOR

One of the easiest ways to begin determining what you truly want is to catalog what you want through visualizing it. This powerful exercise will help you create your ultimate life list. Start by having a friend read the following prompts to you (or audio-record it yourself in a slow, soothing voice; then listen to it with your eyes closed). If you record it, be sure to pause in between each category so you'll have time to write down your answers.

Begin by listening to some relaxing music and sitting quietly in a comfortable environment. Close your eyes. Then, begin visualizing your ideal life exactly as if you are living it.

1. First, visualize your financial situation. How much money do you have in your savings? How much do you make in annual income? What's your net worth? How about your cash flow?

2. Next, visualize your possessions. What does your home look like? Where is it located? What color are the rooms? Are there paintings hanging on the walls? What do they look like? Walk through your perfect house visually, using your mind's eye.

At this point, don't worry about how you'll get that house. Don't sabotage yourself by saying, "I can't live in Hawaii because I don't make enough money." Once you give your mind's eye the picture, your mind will solve the not-enough-money challenge. Simply be honest with yourself about what you truly want.

Next, visualize what kind of car you're driving and the other possessions you own and enjoy. Open your eyes and write down what you see, in great detail. Or give a friend exact details to jot down.

3. Next, visualize your career. What are you doing in your career? Where are you working? Whom are you working with? What kind of clients are you serving? What is your compensation like? Is it your own business?

4. Then, focus on your free time and recreation. What are you doing with your family and friends in the free time you've created for yourself? What hobbies are you pursuing? What kinds of sports are you engaging in? What kinds of vacations do you take?

5. Next, visualize your body, physical health, emotional health, and spiritual life. Are you free and open, relaxed, pain-free, in an ecstatic state of joy all day long? What does that look like?

6. Then, begin visualizing your relationships with your family and friends. What is your relationship with your family like? Who are your friends? What is the quality of your relationships with friends? What do those friendships feel like? Are they loving, supportive, empowering, fun? Could they be better?

7. What about your own personal growth? Do you see yourself going back to school, taking training, seeking therapy or counseling for a past hurt, or growing spiritually?

8. Move on to the community you live in, the community you've chosen. It's ideal, isn't it? What does it look like? Who's in your network? What kinds of community activities take place there? What about your charitable or philanthropic work? What do you do to help others and make a difference? How often do you participate in these activities? Whom are you helping?

Once you decide what you want in each of these eight areas, you can begin to break down your lifestyle *wants* into small, achievable goals that will eventually bring about the ultimate life you want.

This vision will activate your brain to achieve what you want

Extensive study has shown that once we decide what we want, the brain goes to work actually helping us bring about these life-changing results. For instance, experts know that when you give it a goal, the brain triggers its *reticular activating system*—a web of neural pathways that filters through the millions of random images, facts, and information we're bombarded with each day—then sends to our conscious minds those bits of data that will help us achieve our goals.

When you give your brain an image of something you want to achieve, your subconscious will labor around the clock to find ways to achieve the picture you put there. Without a doubt, the brain is a goal-seeking instrument.

BELIEVE YOU WILL SUCCEED

Now that you've decided what you want in life, the next most obvious step is to *believe it's possible*—not only for someone else to achieve those outcomes *but for you to do so.*

Think about it.

In the course of pursuing your goals, you'll be expending Herculean amounts of energy. You'll be dedicating serious time. You'll likely need to educate yourself on new processes, form new relationships, and even learn new skills and habits. It's pretty unlikely that you'd do all those things if you *didn't believe* your outcome was possible, right?

So believing your desires are possible to achieve is an important first step.

But even more important than that, believing that *you can achieve those goals* is what's so critical to this equation.

> Believe it can be done. When you believe something can be done, really believe, your mind will find the ways to do it. Believing a solution paves the way to solution.
>
> —DAVID J. SCHWARTZ
> AUTHOR OF *THE MAGIC OF THINKING BIG*

To strengthen your belief that your goals are possible, begin by seeking out examples of individuals who have already achieved goals similar to yours. Learn from their experiences. While your breakthrough goals may be challenging for you, realize that count-less others have already succeeded at what you want to do. Invest time discovering stories of those people who have accomplished what you aspire to achieve.

Where are good places to look for these stories?

Magazines, podcasts, documentaries, and online videos will introduce you to people who've succeeded—in fact, they often show *exactly* how those achievers accomplished what you want to do. Some of my favorite resources are *Entrepreneur, Inc.*, and *Wired* magazines; television shows like Oprah's *Super Soul Sunday*, *Shark Tank*, or *CNN Heroes*; and podcasts like *How I Built This*, *Eventual Millionaire*, and *The School of Greatness*. All these share tales of individuals who started from humble beginnings and rose to prominence.

As you consume these stories, you'll expand your perception of what's achievable for an individual. Witnessing the triumphs of ordinary people who believed in themselves and worked toward their goals reinforces the idea that success is within reach for anyone.

> If we did all the things we are capable of doing, we would literally astound ourselves.
>
> —Thomas Edison
> One of America's greatest inventors

Once you recognize that others have already achieved what you desire, the next crucial step is believing that you can do it too. This shift in mindset is indispensable to your success. In fact, the key to self-confidence and belief in oneself lies in recognizing that we can choose what to believe. Belief is a choice! You absolutely have the power to *decide to believe* you can achieve your goals.

Take a moment to pause and make the decision right now to believe in your ability to accomplish your biggest goals. It might seem like a simple step, but this "I can do it" decision is the foundation of your journey toward success. You don't need to know *how you'll achieve your goals* at this point; you just need to decide that you can...and you will.

Eliminate Limiting Beliefs

Of course, once you embark on your goal-achieving journey, old beliefs that can limit you—mentally and even physically—will begin to emerge. These usually appear as limiting thoughts that creep in, just as you're about to take action.

"I want this, but..." is a common one. Or your internal critic will tell you *you're not smart enough, rich enough, or pretty enough.*

You might actually think you don't deserve the outcomes you want. Your limiting beliefs—often rooted in childhood, then reinforced through early adulthood experiences—hinder your progress by reinforcing the idea that certain things are not possible for you.

To break free from these constraints, you need to acknowledge and challenge these beliefs. Choose to write down and repeat the opposite thoughts anytime the negative ones come up. Recognize that they're often based on falsehoods and, at the same time, are obstacles that can be overcome.

Believing in yourself is a choice. Make the decision now to believe you can *be, do,* or *have* anything you want. Then set aside and replace your limiting beliefs, and open the door to the boundless possibilities that await you.

THINK ABUNDANTLY

One of the great strategies for success is to *act as if* you are *already where you want to be*—with all the lifestyle perks, connections, and abundance that goes with it. This means thinking like, talking like, dressing like, acting like, and feeling like the person who has already achieved your goal.

Acting as if sends powerful commands to your subconscious mind to find creative ways to achieve your goals. It programs the *reticular activating system* in your brain to start noticing anything that will help you succeed. And it sends strong messages to the universe that this goal is something you really want.

Start acting as if...

The first time I used this principle was in the late 1970s. I was doing a lot of speaking and training at the time when I happened to meet another seminar leader who had just returned from Australia.

I decided that I too wanted to travel and speak all around the globe.

I asked myself what I would need in order to become an international consultant. I called the passport office and asked them how to apply for one. I purchased a clock that showed all the international time zones. I had business cards printed with the words "international consultant" on them. Finally, I decided that Australia would be the first place I would like to go, so I went to a travel agency and got a huge travel poster featuring the Sydney Opera House, Ayers Rock, and a kangaroo-crossing sign. Every morning while I ate my breakfast, I looked at that poster on my refrigerator and imagined being in Australia.

Less than a year later I was invited to conduct seminars in Sydney and Brisbane in Australia. As soon as I started acting as if I were an international consultant, the universe responded by treating me like one—the powerful law of attraction at work.

Be, do, and have everything you want...starting now.

You can begin right now to act as if you've already achieved any goal you desire, and that *outer experience* of *acting as if* will create the *inner experience*—the success mindset—that will lead you to the actual manifestation of that experience.

Once you choose what you want to be, do, or have, all you have to do is start acting as if you already are being, doing, or having it.

For instance, how would you act if you were already a top salesperson, a highly paid consultant, a rich entrepreneur, a world-class athlete, a best-selling author, an internationally acclaimed artist, a sought-after speaker, or a celebrated actor or musician? How would you think, talk, act, carry yourself, dress, treat other people, handle money, eat, live, travel, and so forth?

Once you have a clear picture of that, start being it...now!

Successful people exude self-confidence, ask for what they want, and say what they don't want. They think anything is possible, take risks, and celebrate their successes. They save a portion of their income and share a portion with others. You too can do all these things right now—before you ever become rich and successful. These things don't cost money, just intention. And as soon as you start acting as if, you'll start drawing to you the very people, resources, and opportunities that will help you achieve it in real life.

Remember, the proper order of things is to start now and *be* who you want to be, then *do* the actions that go along with being that person, and soon you will find that you easily *have* everything you want in life—health, wealth, and fulfilling relationships.

FOCUS ON CREATING THE LIFE YOU WANT

It's been said that in life you get what you focus on. This rule applies to learning a new skill, creating better relationships, or earning more money—virtually any goal or experience you can envision for yourself.

So how can you maintain a *mindset of focus* when working toward achieving your goals? Here are a few tips that work:

Practice The Rule of 5.

When Mark Victor Hansen and I first published *Chicken Soup for the Soul*, our goal was to create a *New York Times* number one best seller. With that goal in mind, we interviewed dozens of book-marketing experts and sought the advice of numerous best-selling authors. After receiving literally hundreds of strategies we could pursue, to be honest, our goal started to seem a little overwhelming.

Then one day we were talking to a friend who reminded us that even the largest tree could be felled simply by swinging an ax at its trunk just five times a day. "Eventually," he concluded, "the tree will have to come down, no matter how large."

Out of that advice, we developed what we called The Rule of 5:

doing five simple things every single day that will move you closer to completing your goal.

In the case of *Chicken Soup for the Soul*, it meant doing five radio interviews a day. Or sending out five review copies to newspapers every day. Or asking five pastors to use a story from the book in their sermons. Or calling five companies to buy a copy for all their workers. Or sending five press releases a day. And on and on...every day for more than two years.

Maintain a bias for action.

Many people have had good ideas—some of which have led to entirely new industries or never-before-seen ways of making money. Of course, the internet in its infancy was a place where many people had good ideas. But how many of those people took action and created the Googles, Amazons, Facebooks, Ubers, and other businesses we know today?

The fact is, while most people know a lot about making money or getting results or creating advancement in the world, only a few actually get to enjoy the rewards of this knowledge (whether financial, professional, or otherwise)—simply because the rest don't take action on their ideas.

Successful people, on the other hand, have a bias for action.

More than any other characteristic, action is what separates the successful from the unsuccessful—the people who actually reap the rewards from those who would merely like to.

Perhaps you too had a great idea at one time—only to see it turned into a successful business or a new invention or a popular product or a new service by someone else because they took action and you did not.

The reality is that, in the world today, the people who are rewarded are those who take action. We're paid for what we do.

Plan your day the night before.

Here's a habit that will help you hit the ground running every morning and get closer to your goals: plan your five must-do items the night before. By jotting down your priorities and tasks the night before, you'll also reduce "decision fatigue" and boost productivity too. And if you need to research how to tackle a task, you can do that the night before, allowing you to focus on execution the next day instead of getting stuck in figuring out what needs to be done.

Another trick is to schedule specific blocks of time in your calendar for each activity rather than to just work from a to-do list.

Finally, follow your joy and focus on being happy.

One final principle—a mindset that I believe is the *real key* to happiness—is to let go of judgments about how other people and situations should be. Most of our pain is from trying to control things we can't while believing that other people and conditions should be different than they are.

When I give up judging and trying to control others, and instead focus on creating what I want for me, I stop resisting reality and find an inner peace from which I can more effortlessly create.

Think of happiness and joy not only as an end state to be sought after but also as an internal guidance system that we are all endowed with. Every one of us was born with an infallible way of knowing what is for our highest good. We just have to tune in to what we are feeling. And if we're not feeling love, joy, peace, and ease, that is nature's way of telling us we're off course. Instead, follow your heart, follow your passions, and do what you love.

About Jack

Known as America's number one success coach, Jack Canfield is the founder and chairman of The Canfield Training Group in Santa Barbara, California, which trains and coaches entrepreneurs, corporate leaders, managers, sales professionals, educators, and the general public in how to accelerate the achievement of their personal, professional, and financial goals.

Jack is best known as the coauthor of the number one *New York Times* best-selling Chicken Soup for the Soul® book series, which has sold more than six hundred million books in forty-nine languages, including forty-one *New York Times* best sellers.

As the CEO of Chicken Soup for the Soul Enterprises, he helped grow the Chicken Soup for the Soul® brand into a virtual empire of books, children's books, audios, videos, CDs, classroom materials, a syndicated column, and a television show, as well as a vigorous program of licensed products that includes everything from clothing and board games to nutraceuticals and a successful line of Chicken Soup for the Pet Lover's Soul® cat and dog foods.

His other books include *The Success Principles™: How to Get from Where You Are to Where You Want to Be* (now available in its 10th Anniversary Edition); *The Success Principles™ Workbook*; *The Success Principles for Teens*; *The Aladdin Factor*; *Dare to Win*; *Heart at Work*; *The Power of Focus: How to Hit Your Business, Personal and Financial Targets with Confidence and Certainty*; *You've Got to Read This Book!*; *Tapping into Ultimate Success*; Jack Canfield's Key to Living the Law of Attraction; *The 30-Day Sobriety Solution*; and his recent autobiographical novel, *The Golden Motorcycle Gang: A Story of Transformation.*

Jack is a dynamic speaker and was inducted into the National Speakers Association's Speaker Hall of Fame. He has appeared on more than one thousand radio and television shows, including *The Oprah Winfrey Show, The Montel Williams Show, Larry King Live, The Today Show, Fox and Friends*, and two different hour-long *PBS Specials* devoted exclusively to his work. Jack is also a featured teacher in twelve movies, including *The Secret, The Meta Secret, The Truth, The Keeper of the Keys, Tapping the Source*, and *The Tapping Solution*. Jack was also honored with a documentary produced about his life and teachings called *The Soul of Success: The Jack Canfield Story.*

Jack has personally helped hundreds of thousands of people on six continents become multimillionaires, business leaders, best-selling authors, leading sales professionals, successful entrepreneurs, and world-class athletes while at the same time creating balanced, fulfilling, and healthy lives.

His corporate clients have included Virgin Records, Sony Pictures, Daimler-Chrysler, Federal Express, GE, Johnson & Johnson, Microsoft, Merrill Lynch, Campbell's Soup, Re/Max, the Million Dollar Forum, the Million Dollar Roundtable, the Young Entrepreneurs' Organization, the Young Presidents' Organization, the Executive Committee, and the World Business Council.

He is the founder of the Transformational Leadership Council and a member of Evolutionary Leaders, two groups devoted to helping create a world that works for everyone.

Jack is a graduate of Harvard, earned his MEd from the University of Massachusetts, and has received three honorary doctorates in psychology and public service. He is married and has three children, two stepchildren, and two grandsons.

For more information, visit www.JackCanfield.com.

CHAPTER 2

MY PATH OF RESILIENCE

Wisdom for Making It Happen Despite Hard Times

By Salintae Tuzo-Smith

"I need the doctor to see my daughter right away."

"I'm sorry, ma'am. If you don't have an appointment, the doctor is booked solid and unavailable now."

My mother wouldn't take no for an answer. "I won't leave until the doctor sees my daughter." She waited outside the doctor's office in the sickle cell unit for him to be done—till the end of the day—then barged into the office.

"I can't see you, ma'am," he said.

Willing to go to any lengths to help me, she then laid an envelope of cash on his desk from my parents' emergency fund and said, "I don't care what it takes," demanding for me to be seen. "Please save her leg."

"Take the cash back. I'll see what I can do."

That moment changed my life.

THE PAINFUL BEGINNING

As a child born in the vast expanse of Canada, where my father, Clinton Smith, attended university, my formative years unfolded in the tranquil shores of Bermuda. It was there, at a mere three months of age, I was diagnosed with sickle cell disease. My childhood was punctuated by incessant cries and recurrent health challenges ushering me in and out of hospital corridors and through a relentless quest for answers, eluding even the most astute of physicians. When a blood test confirmed the presence of sickle cell anemia disease, the veil of uncertainty began to lift.

My early years were full of painful episodes. A symphony of discomfort frequently led me from the classroom to the sterile confines of hospital rooms. Pneumonia, an unwelcome visitor, made repeated visits into my young life, disrupting the semblance of normalcy with its unwavering persistence. Simple things like, "Drink your water; get your rest," became quite a task for my devoted mother, Suzette Tuzo, to enforce in a young child.

The agony of sickle cell disease is relentless. Morphine and codeine, reliable companions in the battle against pain even for adults, offered some respite while the prospect of blood transfusions loomed to help add healthy blood and bring me out of painful episodes.

The intricate dance of sickle cell disease unfolds as cells lose their oxygen, contorting into ominous shapes impeding the flow of blood throughout the body. Blockages ensue, oxygen is withheld, and the body reels from the onslaught of pain, strokes, and/or organ failure.

During one particular visit to the hospital when I was three, having been in and out of the hospital so much and always getting an IV, they couldn't find the veins in my arms or hands, so they put an IV in my foot.

Due to negligence, the IV slipped out of the vein, and the fluid filled my foot. My mother woke up to me screaming as my foot split open.

The doctor in Bermuda, faced with the gravity of the situation, delivered a somber verdict: my foot and leg were on the verge of amputation. In the face of despair, my mother's resolve remained unshaken.

"Absolutely not. No way," my mother said adamantly to the doctor. She was determined to take me overseas, hoping for a different outcome, and we headed to Toronto.

FACING THE BATTLES WITH A POSITIVE MINDSET

With the new doctor's commitment to salvaging my foot, I had to quarantine with my mother, in a room only fit for a toddler, for a few days in the hospital before he could perform the surgery. A skin graft, sourced from the expanse of my upper thigh, became the unlikely hero, and the outcome was successful. I always joke and say I have butt skin on my foot.

Grateful for his intervention, I found myself with many obstacles to surmount. As a three-year-old, I had to relearn how to walk.

As I grew older, I avoided pool parties, haunted by the insecurity of showing my "monster foot." I often missed out on things other kids could do. This affected my mindset and outlook on life at an early age and would later become a major hurdle to overcome.

I've always had issues with my leg—I even had surgery as a teenager to slow down the growth in my left leg so it would be more comparable to my right leg. My legs are uneven in both length and girth. My ubiquitous limp became a part of me with the aid of lifts.

I recall a pivotal moment in gym class when we had to run one mile—four laps around the building, a seemingly insurmountable challenge for someone with leg ailments like me. After three laps, I stopped. I always tried to do my best and push as much as possible, but my leg had no muscle, and it was hard to keep up.

"I can't do this," I cried.

"Yes, you can," said my gym coach.

He was unaware of the extent to which my leg affected me. I did my best to hide the struggle and tried to compensate to blend in.

I learned a life lesson on that day: *While you may disappoint someone else, you're not disappointing yourself!* As I grew older, I began to understand while there is pressure in letting others down, the real measure of your personal worth lies in your own self-respect.

I was bullied in school. I remember not wanting to leave the car one morning because I saw a boy standing there. "Why don't you want to get out of the car?" my mother asked. "Does he bully you?"

"Yes."

I always made it known I was smart and quick with my words in an effort to discourage kids from bullying me. I had to build a tough exterior to get ahead of the bullies.

"What's wrong with your leg?" was a common question, not always out of malicious intent or bullying but still hard to navigate, especially as a kid.

Truthfully, I was my worst bully. As I matured, I learned your scars are something to be proud of because they're something you've overcome. You've conquered those things; they didn't conquer you! Everyone battles insecurity on some level. If I didn't have issues with my leg, I would've been insecure about something else. I wasn't alone. We all battle insecurity. Gaining this valuable perspective was a powerful motivator and catalyst for my mindset to develop in healthy ways.

But my mindset would only hold positive for so long. Eventually, the battle persisted, and discouragement continued to creep in. In my late twenties I wanted to commit suicide. I was in and out of the hospital many times within a year. I was physically, mentally, and emotionally exhausted, and I wanted to end it all. I wanted to overdose on the morphine the hospital prescribed.

I did the right thing and reached out to my closest friends and let them know about my struggle. I wasn't feeling it anymore; I wasn't feeling life. After they tried to speak sense and love into me, I made a last-ditch effort and prayed.

While praying, a scene played in my mind where I was hanging off a cliff, and as I reached up with my last bit of energy, I touched the hem of Jesus' garment. It reminded me of the story in the Bible where the woman with the issue of blood touched Jesus' garment while in a large crowd.

I felt seen. Prayer worked. I felt an ounce of hope and was able to start reflecting on the possibility of life after the pain. After sourcing encouragement and God's power through my friends, I asked myself, "Are you going to commit suicide or not? If not, are you going to live in a spiral of despair, or will you change it?"

You have to make a conscious decision to change your path. The more your mindset improves around what's happening, the more your situation improves. If you take one step forward in your mental clarity, your situation improves one step. Otherwise, your situation won't get better but will get even worse. We either progress or regress, but we don't stay still.

If you change nothing, you are likely going backward as you sit and dwell in despair. Who wants that? Not me! I had had enough, and I didn't want it anymore.

It's not easy, but it becomes easier once you make the choice. It's OK to slow down and focus on surviving before thriving.

As an adult, I could never wear high heels—and as a woman, I felt robbed. Heels are the pinnacle of fashion for so many. All my friends wore heels, and something so seemingly insignificant made me feel *less than* all the time.

I had to accept this reality, which felt harsh, but it was necessary. Though it made me feel less attractive than my counterparts, I realized *people would have to get to know me for me*. In a way, I realized and believed God was protecting me from people and situations that could have hurt me. It's the little things that often have major impacts on our lives.

I often wondered, "What would my life be like if I didn't have this leg issue? Would I be considered more beautiful, strutting my stuff because the boys want to holler? Could this have been a distraction for me?"

Growing up, my brother was great at sports. My daughter is great at sports. Eventually, I had to accept I wouldn't be an athlete. Sometimes it's easier to accept harsh realities in order to see a better perspective within your realm. I've learned when we let go of what is not meant for us, sometimes even greater things will come! What we may see as a drawback can often be a better path for our lives.

No matter what you are going through, there's always a positive perspective to be found! Sometimes you really have to search for it, but it's always there. The answer usually lies in our mindset.

"God gives his hardest battles to his strongest soldiers," my mother would often say to me growing up. She may not have realized it at the time, but her statement carried me through many difficult times, giving me hope that I could overcome no matter how hard it felt at the time.

Every time we face a battle, we think it's our worst one yet—but we get through it. I have. "This too shall pass," my mother says.

My dad was not available as much for me medically, but I owe my bubbly spirit and optimism to him. I never remember my dad in a bad mood.

"Listen. Don't take life too seriously, and don't worry," he said, assuring me "it's going to be OK."

A parent's power to impact the mindset of their children should never be underestimated. These truths from my parents gave me the resolve and the mindset to get through anything I've had to face.

THE FAITH FACTOR

My unwavering faith has been the cornerstone of my journey toward overcoming adversity, nowhere more evident than during my pregnancy.

When the news of my pregnancy entered my life, the circumstances were far from ideal. The father and I were in the fledgling stages of our relationship and found ourselves at a crossroads. He had children and didn't want another. Instead, he wanted me to terminate the pregnancy. The hematologist also wanted me to terminate the pregnancy considering the struggles of people with sickle cell. There was a 50 percent chance my child would have it too. There's a test you can take to find out ahead of time, but it didn't matter to me because I was not going to terminate the pregnancy.

The decision lay not within the realm of mortal judgment but in the divine providence of a higher power. Despite the pressures and pleas surrounding me, I remained resolute in my belief: the fate of this precious life lay beyond the realm of human intervention.

In the face of skepticism and opposition, I sought solace in prayer, my unwavering trust in the divine guiding me through a sea of uncertainty. With each passing day, I nurtured the life growing within me, cocooned in the protective embrace of my faith and resolve.

I prayed about it and hoped God was going to bless me and be with my child. In an effort to protect my mind and my boundaries, I kept my pregnancy a secret for five months. I had to do what was best for me and the baby.

I set my mind to think positively. Every day, I sang the Lauryn Hill song "To Zion," choosing my child over my career and the opinions of others. I did prenatal yoga as much as I could, and I received a blood transfusion once every trimester. Each morning, my routine involved a new conversation with positive affirmations to myself.

Thankfully, when my child was born, there was no sign of sickle cell! My daughter is a symbol and reminder of my faith. *Through the power of faith, you can overcome anything.* But again, you have to make a choice in order to make it happen: faith over fear.

METANOIA POWER

My journey has been a profound lesson in the power of resilience and the indomitable strength of the human spirit to triumph over life's adversities.

Today, as a chronic illness coach, I walk alongside individuals, helping them reshape their perspectives on their own ailments, and I hold a master's degree in Christian counseling. I believe your relationship with God matters more than anything. Our personal relationship with Jesus sustains us in the darkest moments, igniting the flame of hope within our souls. This ember in our hearts must be nurtured and kept alive.

My counseling and coaching venture is named Metanoia Power (www.metanoiapower.com). The name embodies the essence of transformation—a shift in mindset born from the despair of breakdown and a conscious choice to chart a new course. My practice is a beacon of hope, a sanctuary for those seeking refuge from the storms of life.

I am committed to equipping individuals with the tools they need to advocate for themselves and reclaim their lives in the face of illness and other struggles. From online courses to customizable templates for doctor's visits, my aim is to empower others to find their voice and assert their needs with clarity and conviction.

I have met so many people burdened by illness while shackled by silence and uncertainty. I want to help them remember, "No one knows your body better than you do." Your voice, your truth deserves to be heard and honored.

As I learned to do, I want to help others press through their pain. It begins with a shift in mindset and a belief that even in the darkest storms lies the promise of a better tomorrow.

About Salintae

Salintae is one of the most optimistic individuals you could meet despite the chronic illness she has lived with since birth. Doctors said she wouldn't live past thirty years old, but that did not stop her from traveling the world, earning a master's degree in Christian counseling, becoming a Trauma Informed Certified Coach, or spending close to ten years in the corporate world as a business continuity professional, earning a Certified Business Continuity Professional designation.

Resiliency has always been Salintae's forte, in all areas of her life, and her goal is to reach those who believe they cannot bounce back or have a hard time doing so. Salintae helps her clients transform into people who are more than their illnesses. She inspires them to know they can and teaches them how to manage their mindset despite their circumstances or illnesses.

If her story resonates, you would like additional support, or you would just like to see what she is up to, you can find Salintae at www.meta-noiapower.com or info@metanoiapower.com.

CHAPTER 3

FAILURE ISN'T FINAL— IT'S AN OPPORTUNITY FOR GROWTH

By Max James

Having just rescued a downed fighter pilot out of the mountainous jungles just north of Hanoi in Vietnam, a two-day combat set of missions turned into a nightmare. I got the following call over the intercom from my combat crew chief:

"Captain James, we got a problem back here!"

"What's up, chief? Is that fighter pilot OK?"

"Yes sir, but that's not the problem. We got an oil leak!"

The last thing a helicopter pilot wants to hear in a combat situation is that the transmission is leaking. Enemy fire hadn't killed us, but they did hit the aircraft.

"It's the transmission, Captain!"

I knew immediately my chopper was going down.

The transmission was leaking, which causes the helicopter's rotor blades to stop turning mid-flight. We had only a few seconds, or maybe minutes, before the blades stopped turning altogether and we would fall like a rock.

My stomach began to crawl up my throat. It was closing up, and for a few seconds I wasn't breathing.

My first order was, "Chief, tell the PJ (pararescue specialist) to put a parachute on that pilot. He may have to bail out again!"

The PJ came on the intercom. "Captain James, the pilot has just gone into shock."

That wasn't surprising considering what this fighter jock had endured. He had been shot down either by ground fire or a surface-to-air missile (SAM), parachuted into the side of a mountain through thick jungle trees, and endured a failed rescue attempt the night before. Then he had been chased all night by enemy soldiers before being successfully rescued by our combat crew in our Air Force Jolly Green Giant helicopter at first light the next morning. He survived the ground fire during his ride up the rescue hoist into the chopper, celebrated on board with the crew—and then was told he might have to parachute out again, back down into enemy territory.

Meanwhile, I needed to put the Jolly Green down immediately, but we were over unknown territory, possibly held by enemy forces. I called search-and-rescue (SAR) headquarters in Saigon.

"Mayday, Mayday, Mayday. This is Jolly Green 56 with a serious transmission oil leak. I need to know if there are any safe areas around here so I can set this thing down quickly!"

"Ah, roger, Jolly 56. Understand emergency transmission oil leak and need immediate info on probable safe landing site. Stand by."

"Stand by? Are you kidding me? I don't have time to stand by!"

"Chief, how are we doing back there?" I asked desperately.

"It's getting a hell of a lot worse, sir."

And then over the radio comes, "Jolly Green 56, this is SAR. The following are map coordinates for a village that is about thirty miles from your present position. We think it might be safe to land there."

"What? You think it might be safe?"

"Yes sir. That is the best we can do for you."

Continuing to fly with reduced engine speed and power, we descended slowly toward the coordinates; the gears started to grind slightly as the oil drained from the transmission bed.

Saigon called again: "Jolly Green 56, be prepared that the landing site is a village. We still have reason to believe it's occupied by friendly Laotians."

I wouldn't call what happened a landing...more of a controlled crash, damaging the landing gear and tires, but as they say, any landing that you can walk away from is a good one.

After some very tense minutes, we discovered that the village was indeed friendly as they brought us tea as a gesture of hospitality.

Through my time in Vietnam, I was faced with dozens of rescue missions, but it was the failed rescues that haunted me the most. Jolly Green pilots were there to save lives, not take them.

After any failed attempts in the combat zone, I learned very quickly that my *mindset mattered* more than anything else. Allowing failure to destroy my ability to do my job was not in the realm of possibilities. I was there to serve, so beyond my military training, I was forced to create my own methods for staying resilient, resourceful, and learning from it all.

Because of determination, grit, and preparation, we were far more successful than not. My crews and I were blessed to pick up ten downed pilots during my tour in Vietnam. Ten pilots came home when, without our continuing efforts, their alternatives would have been death or the "Hanoi Hilton" as a prisoner of war. The Jolly Greens brought home about 80 percent of the downed pilots during the war.

I share these experiences and the lessons learned from failure in my book titled *The Harder I Fall, the Higher I Bounce*—it is the mindset I have always tried to live by and one that will also propel you to succeed as an entrepreneur. Failure is never final, as long as you learn from it.

Upon returning from Vietnam, I decided to go to school for my MBA at Stanford University back in the early '70s. My first venture into the entrepreneurial world was called Executorial Services and provided rentable space to entrepreneurs and independent salespeople. It was like WeWork, just forty years ahead of its time.

I was excited and did everything I could to make it work...and yet it failed.

My second business did well and eventually failed. And my fourth and fifth businesses did OK but never really brought me the level of success I was looking for.

No matter how many times I have failed in business or in life, I learned to never take it personally. Instead, I have asked myself the same questions over and over again: "What did I do incorrectly?" Remembering my experience of being shot down in the war, I was quick to ask myself, "Was it me or an outside influence that caused my company to go bust? What should I do differently the next time?"

I truly believe that I was able to learn more, go farther, and be far more successful because I treated my entrepreneurial career as a science experiment. Always questioning. Poking, prodding until I got it right.

Those lessons have become a ubiquitous part of my life, and I am honored to share some of the most important of these lessons on the following pages.

WHEN PREPARATION MEETS OPPORTUNITY, TAKE IT

When I was seventeen I accepted a position in Washington, DC, working for our state congressman. I couldn't believe that I had been chosen to be his administrative assistant.

I was curious at how I could have a career in Washington . . . become a politician, or even president of the United States (a lofty goal at seventeen, I know). I asked him his thoughts on the matter, and his response changed the course of my life that day: "First thing, son, is you have to go to college. Then possibly join the military—to honorably serve your country. People vote for success."

When I informed him that I had dropped out of school so I could stay in DC and work on Capitol Hill, he made one phone call, and suddenly all my classes were sent to me from Humboldt, Tennessee, as a correspondence course. To sweeten the deal, which was unheard of at the time, he promised my high school that I would show up for final exams. Which I did.

When I decided to go to college, he recommended that I go to the newly formed Air Force Academy. He had chosen ten young men to compete for a chance to get into the United States Air Force Academy. I wasn't chosen from this group but still applied anyway. I wasn't accepted.

It turned out that the young men chosen ahead of me excelled in athletic prowess, as well as excellent grades and the right extra-curricular activities and clubs. I had thought that with my connections and the work I was doing, I'd be a shoo-in.

I sulked for a few weeks. But as luck would have it, I didn't really know how the system worked. Many who were chosen for the Air Force Academy simply didn't go, deciding on an alternative college. Therefore, many slots opened up to be filled by qualified alternatives.

A few weeks later I received a letter in the mail informing me that I had been chosen for the academy because an alternate slot became available.

As a qualified alternative do you think I took this second chance lightly? No. I worked harder than most, pushed my own mental and physical boundaries, and took this opportunity and put everything I had in me into succeeding. That worked, apparently, because I received one of the Distinguished Graduates awards upon graduation.

At each step in life, I learned that if I wanted something badly enough, I couldn't just hope for it to happen. I had to take action. If I did, suddenly as if an invisible force paved the way for me, opportunities would just show up. Doors would open. But only if I grabbed that opportunity and went after it.

Patience in the face of setback will serve you well. That doesn't mean you don't get upset. We all do. It just means you may need to give it a day or two to calm down, collect your thoughts, and shift your strategy toward a different goal. Never give up on the dream.

FAILURE IS INEVITABLE—HOW YOU BOUNCE BACK IS YOUR SUPERPOWER

Between 2007 and 2009, the American subprime mortgage crisis hit the United States like a ton of bricks. The vast majority of bundled mortgages had been given triple A ratings despite the potential for 70 percent of the mortgage holders to default on their mortgages.

Several years before the collapse, I had bought seven area franchises from RE/MAX. Although RE/MAX was founded in 1973 by Dave and Gail Liniger, they were really expanding rapidly at the time, and it seemed like a no-brainer to get involved. I mean real estate is always booming, right?

I had the rights to RE/MAX from San Francisco up through Santa Rosa, Sonoma, to Sacramento. We leased offices and hired employees, and I took one office and turned it into nine.

Then the collapse came, and I did everything I could to not lose my expanding business. Most deals at that time were to take care of creditors, keep the leasing company from repossessing their computers and office furniture, while begging for an extension.

This may come as a shock to many of you, but you can do everything right, build an empire, and still have it all collapse through no fault of your own. Outside forces can be devastating and may take over a decade for you to recover from. Just remember, it ain't always your fault.

How you get back up after catastrophic failure is the real key to success. As they say in the martial arts, "Knocked down seven times, get up eight."

ADAPT TO TRENDS IN THE MARKETPLACE

The number one question I get asked on television, radio, or podcast interviews is, "What was it like to be shot down twice in Vietnam?"

Imagine engine failure from a bullet to the transmission fluid line, and suddenly you have to tilt the blades to slow your descent. As you guide the chopper down, avoiding trees and mountainsides, you're also looking for a potential landing spot.

In the pit of your stomach is a ball of fear, but in that moment, you remember your training and take what little action you can in what seems to be a helpless situation.

Now apply that to a start-up. As an entrepreneur you are flying by the seat of your pants. You have to adapt to the changing landscape and question whether it is a fad or a trend.

What do I mean by that? From 1995–2004 the internet as a commerce center was untrusted. Although it appeared to be a fad at first, companies like Netflix started physically shipping DVDs to your home at a time when people were still using VHS tapes. That took a heroic effort to start a business and stay in the fight until people felt comfortable enough to trust purchasing products and services online.

Today, Netflix, Amazon, and YouTube are a ubiquitous part of our daily online landscape.

At American Kiosk Management we were always quick to embrace technology. One of the ways we used this trend was to create customer loyalty campaigns for our main product, Proactiv®. We later branched out to automated retail (aka vending machines), where someone could purchase a Proactiv® kit without the pressure and embarrassment of a sales professional applying the product as hundreds of people walked by our kiosks.

We adapted to the trends and used it to reach a new customer base while supporting potential customers with a buying alternative.

I've lost fortunes, and I've made several fortunes. I even lost my dream house shortly after I moved in. All I can say is this: Staying in the game of life despite one setback after another separates the wannabes from the warriors. Your *mindset matters.*

It's been an honor through the years to help other entrepreneurs and Air Force Academy students and graduates. I feel honored to pass off the baton to the next generation of leaders. And never forget, failure is never final.

About Max

Max James is an American author and serial entrepreneur, best known as the founder of American Kiosk Management Co. and dubbed the King of Kiosks by *Fortune* magazine.

Max is a graduate of the United States Air Force Academy and, after serving as a Jolly Green rescue helicopter pilot in Vietnam, earned an MBA from Stanford University.

Ever since then, Max has built one business after another, and he shares his life's journey in the pages of his award-winning book *The Harder I Fall, the Higher I Bounce*—a business memoir for today's entrepreneurs and business executives.

From growing up on a farm and the life lessons learned through his father, to rescue pilot in Vietnam—shot down twice and lived to tell about it—to building a billion-dollar company from the ground up, Max shares the lessons learned from failure, and the real-world steps it takes to bounce back.

Max is the recipient of the US Air Force Academy's Distinguished Graduate Award and resides with his wife, Linda Johansen-James, in Las Vegas, Nevada.

Learn more: www.maxjamesauthor.com.

CHAPTER 4

WE ARE THE SUM OF THE STORIES WE BELIEVE

By Nick Nanton

"**N**ick, you're so stupid."

I was nine years old, called on by my teacher, frozen in my seat because I didn't have the answer to the next math problem. Or any of the math problems.

"Is my brain just incapable of understanding this stuff? Can she see something about me that I can't? Is multiplication so hard because I'm dumb?"

Later at home, staring at the multiplication grid of numbers 1 through 12, all I felt was daunted. The numbers didn't make sense. "So stupid."

I'm sure my teacher was just having a bad day. Knowing me, I probably was joking around in class trying to get a reaction from my friends. But that experience planted a seed, a mindset about myself, that stuck with me for years. She told me a story about myself that I believed: I can't do math.

A couple of days later, my parents sat me down and explained how in multiplication I didn't have to work out the answers to every problem. I just had to memorize them. Well, now I had a new problem because the idea that I'd be able to memorize all those factors on the grid felt equally impossible.

God bless my parents. They broke it down into manageable parts for me, first telling me to memorize the 1 times; then, a few days later (OK, no, it didn't take me a few days to learn the row of ones; I wasn't that clueless), I'd move on to 2 times, and on and on until, a few weeks later, I felt comfortable in my math class doing the problems like the other students.

Truthfully, I probably would have ended up hating math for some other reason, so I give my teacher grace because everyone says things they don't mean. Still, she ruined the idea of math for me for the rest of my life. Later on, after I'd won an Emmy, I would joke that I wanted to ship a box of Emmys to her door with a note that said, "How stupid am I now?" But that was me allowing her to live rent-free in my head. Funnily enough, I know she doesn't remember saying that to me, because when she sees my mother in the grocery store, she tells her, "Nicky was always one of my favorite students."

Everybody remembers a moment when a teacher, parent, or coach said something that planted a seed of insecurity inside them. People make offhanded comments all the time with no idea that their words may have just cut someone to their soul.

Our mindsets are a culmination of what we've lived through and what we choose to believe about what others have said about us. We become the sum of the stories we believe about ourselves. We bring those stories into every encounter we have. In that sense, everything we do begins with mindset.

For instance, I recently read a story in *The Guardian* written by a guy who believed his father was Native American, but a recent DNA test revealed a surprise. His father had adopted a new identity after doing jail time, rejecting his Chinese-African American lineage and telling people, including his wife and young children, that he was Native American. He writes how he has since tried to cope with losing part of his identity. "I was already in my thirties when my Indianness was pulled out from under me. It had taken me years to settle what I thought about race."

Here's another scenario. Imagine a woman was adopted but didn't know it. The women in her family have a history of getting early-onset dementia, so at age fifty-five, after she notices a growing forgetfulness, she's convinced she too has the illness. She goes to her mother and shares her concern, only to learn the truth about her adoption.

The good news is that the stories we believe about ourselves aren't written in stone. We get to choose how we'll respond to what others say about us.

Let's do a little activity to find out what stories you believe about yourself. Grab a sheet of paper or open up a new screen, and list out the ten most crucial moments of your life—positive and negative. Put a star next to the ones that negatively impacted you. Now, think about how you could go at the painful event from a different perspective.

I'll go first.

My teacher told me I was stupid. (Negative)

That inspired in me a drive to study as long as it took to prove her words wrong. (A positive take on the event)

Here's another one (not about me, but you get the point): That toxic relationship in college ruined me for love for all of my twenties. (Negative)

If I hadn't been so burned by that relationship in college, I may not have waited so long to settle down. I may have missed marrying my best friend in my thirties. (Positive take)

Ultimately, rewriting your past is not lying to yourself but reframing it to protect yourself from what you allow to live rent-free in your mind. If another person's hurtful words start a shaming narrative about who we believe we are, we miss out on the future opportunities we don't think we're qualified to have. Every situation has the potential of a positive outcome simply from the mindset you choose to accept about it.

The person who was told they were part Native American may feel a more significant loss of identity, even a little death to part of themselves, because of how long that belief had to take root and grow. But look at it from another perspective: this new information opens up a gap now that is fillable, now that they know they aren't Native American. But what is their real heritage? Maybe their lineage comes from Gen. George Patton, Abraham Lincoln, or Lewis and Clark. New stories are waiting to be discovered.

———◆———

Over the years, my mindset has been the catalyst for some pretty wild adventures. I've been part of projects that took me to the streets of Haiti with Navy SEALs and into refugee camps in Iraq. I've had the privilege of working with incredible, inspiring people.

Here are some of the ways I get my mindset in the right place before I go after a big opportunity.

PREPARATION

In life, success starts with preparation. I play out in my mind all the different scenarios I can think of as to how the meeting could go and ways I'll respond. I may even role-play possible conversations until I feel totally confident that I'm ready. Preparation is vital.

I used to feel like I had to have the best idea in the room, but then I learned something from a songwriting buddy of mine. When he first invited me in Nashville, he told me, "Hey, you're talented and you're also really young. I'm gonna put you in a room with me and the other writers. We've all been writing two hundred to three hundred songs a year for the last decade. Your experience cannot stack up to that. So while I want you to bring great ideas, and fight for what's great, your goal is not to have the best idea in the room. Your goal is to bring whatever you bring so the best song gets written in the room that day. It's not about your idea. It's not even about their ideas. It's about what's the best collaboration we can all have."

Wow, that was a valuable experience. Now I prepare for the best conversation that day based on what I know, and that doesn't mean I just wing it. I do my research on who they are and what they like, and the projects they've done that went well. (Confession: I actually hate doing research, so I outsource it and get a brief on what I should know.)

Visualization

Another tool I use is visualization. There is so much to be said for positive beliefs. I use visualization to envision what winning will look like. Athletes at the top of their game practice this. I read a *New York Times* article about the Canadian bobsledder and Olympic medalist Lyndon Rush. He said before he arrived in Sochi, Russia, for the Winter Olympics, he'd been training there mentally for months. "I've tried to keep the track in my mind throughout the year. I'll be in the shower or brushing my teeth. It just takes a minute, so I do the whole thing or sometimes just the corners that are more technical. You try to keep it fresh in your head so when you do get there, you are not just starting at square one. It's amazing how much you can do in your mind."

Visualize a successful outcome. Then go into the meeting believing you've already won the medal.

Gratitude

If you aren't finding much joy in your life, check your mindset. Of course, not every second of every day will be the most amazing ever, but you can't be creative if you're not in a state of gratitude, and you can't be in a state of gratitude if you're miserable.

If there's an area of your life that you're not happy about, that's a telltale sign that you're probably not looking at it in the most helpful way. If you're relying on your boss to change or your girlfriend to change, you might be telling yourself an unrealistic story. Not to sound harsh, but maybe it's not everyone else that's failing you. At some point, someone like Larry King, who's been married eight times to seven women, may think, "Maybe it's me."

Try to find more gratitude for the gifts in your life, even in a difficult situation. Take a different perspective and see one good thing that came from what seemed like a disaster. A positive attitude is one of those invisible traits most successful people have in common.

Ask for feedback.

Ask the people you trust for input after a failed situation. This is especially helpful for newer leaders. Echo chambers are never helpful. When you ask for input, be prepared for what you're about to hear. Get ready for super honesty. This is where the term *growing pains* comes from. If a meeting goes poorly, listen to your trusted circle if they suggest you could have gone about things another way with a better result. Check your pride and be open.

Assume you're responsible.

One of my good friends and mentors, Jack Canfield, author of *Chicken Soup for the Soul*, in his book *The Success Principles*™, offers this: Act as if you're responsible.

Let's say the worst-case scenario happens, and you lose a deal or your company tanks. When you get burned, whether in business or in life, it's usually because you either weren't paying attention or were telling yourself a story that wasn't true. Maybe you thought, "I'm better than him; I've covered all my bases; I've done all the research. I trust my gut." Here's an opportunity to say, "What more could I have done?"

Analyze the situation and ask, "How could I have been responsible for this?" Look at all the ways you could have done better due diligence. Even if you can't find anything, delve forward in a proactive way. Ask, "What can I do next time to set more safeguards?" Were you given information you assumed was true, and it turned out not to be? As one of my friends, who's a sheriff, says, "Trust people, but verify." You'll keep yourself out of a lot of trouble by doing that. Next time, check references. Or go to the factory to see the work being done. There's always more you can do to verify the assumptions are true.

Know your individual gifts.

Success boils down to one thing: Be who you are. We all have a skill or talent that sets us apart from the crowd. Dan Sullivan, founder of The Strategic Coach, talks about Unique Ability® being the one thing in life that God put us on earth to do. I'm not talking about running a business. That's not unique. Business management is a bunch of micro skills. What gifting do you bring to the table that no one else in the room brings?

Over the years, I've learned my gift is having meaningful conversations that lead to produced outcomes. When I make documentaries, I have meaningful conversations with my editor, my story producer, the subjects of the film, everybody off camera, the behind-the-scenes crew, and then I let each person do their job to produce the desired outcome. I don't need to wear all the hats or be the expert in the room. I just need to trust that everyone is working within their individual giftings. And if they aren't, that becomes pretty obvious.

Do you know what skill or talent sets you apart from other people? Are you utilizing it in your interactions with those around you?

———•———

These are some mindsets that have helped me grow as a husband, father, and entrepreneur. It starts with getting our mindsets in the right place for us to receive success. Mindsets are formed by the stories we accumulate throughout our lives and how we choose to understand those stories. If we've allowed negative thoughts to shape our mindsets, we walk into a room with shoulders hunched, eyes diverted.

But by finding the positive perspective of those crucial stories, we can shake off insecurities and become leaders who learn from their mistakes. We flip the script that we're too stupid to learn to being someone who loves to learn, but by full immersion, not by sitting behind a desk. We all have something we're especially good at doing. If you bring that to the table, you'll walk into the room with your spine straight and chin up.

If you take just one thing away from this chapter, hold on to this: You have the ability to go back and rewrite your story in a positive way. Look back at the list of ten critical moments. Consider the knowledge you gained of those experiences, and I bet you'll find commonalities among the situations you thrived in, as well as where your weaknesses lie and what you tend to fall for that you probably shouldn't fall for anymore.

When you catch on to these patterns, you'll be able to protect yourself from running after the wrong things and snag the opportunities where your individual gifts are in demand and valued.

Our mindsets are based on the stories we believe about ourselves. If we keep replaying a tragedy in our minds, there's no room for gratitude, joy, or confident leadership. We are not powerless. Quite the opposite. We control what we choose to believe. We become the sum of the stories we believe. Focus on the good, and goodness will surely come.

About Nick

From the slums of Port-au-Prince, Haiti, with special forces raiding a sex trafficking ring and freeing children, to the Virgin Galactic Space Port in Mojave with Sir Richard Branson, twenty-two-time Emmy Award–winning Director-Producer Nick Nanton has become known for telling stories that connect. Why? Because he focuses on the most fascinating subject in the world: *people*. As an award-winning songwriter, storyteller, and best-selling author, Nick has shared his message with millions of people through his documentaries, speeches, blogs, lectures, songs, and best-selling books. Nick's book *StorySelling* hit The Wall Street Journal Best-Seller List and is available on Audible as an audiobook. Nick has directed more than sixty documentaries and a sold-out Broadway Show (garnering forty-three Emmy nominations in multiple regions and twenty-two wins), including:

- *DICKIE V* (ESPN/Disney+)
- *Rudy Ruettiger: The Walk On* (Amazon Prime)
- *The Rebound* (Netflix)
- *Operation Toussaint* (Amazon Prime)

Nick has shared the stage with, coauthored books with, and made films featuring:

- Larry King
- Kathie Lee Gifford
- Hoda Kotb
- Dick Vitale
- Kenny Chesney
- Magic Johnson
- Coach Mike Krzyzewski
- Jack Nicklaus
- Tony Robbins
- Lisa Nichols
- Peter Diamandis
- And many more

Nick specializes in bringing the element of human connection to every viewer, no matter the subject. He is currently directing and hosting the series *In Case You Didn't Know* (season 1 executive produced by Larry King), featuring legends in the worlds of business, entrepreneurship, personal development, technology, and sports.

Nick's first love has always been music. He has been writing songs for more than two decades, and his songs have been aired on radio across the United States and in Canada. He is currently ranked in the top 10 percent of songwriters in the world. His songs have been recorded by Lee Brice, Darius Rucker, RaeLynn, Joe Bryson, and many more, and have amassed more than three million streams on Spotify, Apple Music, Pandora, and SoundCloud. He received three Gold records in 2018 for his work with the global touring band A Day to Remember.

Nick has written and/or produced songs that have appeared on the following shows or in promotional commercials for:

- the Fox prime-time series *Glee, New Girl, House,* and *Hell's Kitchen*
- the MLB All-Star Game
- ABC Family's hit series *Falcon Beach*
- the CBS prime-time series *Ghost Whisperer* starring Jennifer Love Hewitt

CHAPTER 5

A GENUINE, MORE GENEROUS LIFE

Crafting a New Narrative of Success

By Suzanne Nakano

C *lang! Clang! Clang!*
Our manager, Dave, vigorously rang the big copper bell on the wall and yelled for everyone in our one-thousand-square-foot real estate office to hear: "Bill made another sale for this month!" And we clapped as he wrote the sale on the eight-by-ten-foot whiteboard with a squeaky red marker.

There was also the Steak-or-Beans company dinner. Those who achieved their sales goal were awarded a barbecued steak. Those who didn't were recognized with a can of pork 'n' beans and were playfully but publicly shamed.

Did these bell-ringing and steak tactics facilitate real success or simply push us to make more money for the company?

Dave taught us how-to-close-the-sale techniques, and we practiced them with each other. I felt uncomfortable with this sales method, and when I used it with a client, she asked, "Are you practicing closing techniques on me?" *Argh.* At that moment, I realized I didn't want to do what I considered unnatural interactions with people. Selling real estate was my first job after college. Not knowing any better, I reluctantly tried to conform to the company's sales practices for a few years.

Then, one day, I had lunch with colleagues who told me about agents in our office who got caught withholding a material fact about a property for fear the buyer would not buy the property or would pay less for it, and representing both buyer and seller without full disclosure of the meaning of dual representation and the agent receiving more commissions for this type of representation.

The agents who prioritized their sales numbers and income over their clients' best interests increased their risk of paying the price of claims and fines, lost time trying to rectify the situation with clients, and lost reputation.

My internal alarm told me this business duplicity wasn't me. The buildup of discomfort from this real estate job fueled my commitment to maintaining qualities that some of the people I worked with occasionally lacked: integrity, excellence, and a sincere caring for others. Yet more than just these conflicts of morality versus unprincipled behavior helped me form my narrative of success.

Real estate entities that recently settled excessive-fee-charge lawsuits by agreeing to pay millions of dollars in damages confirmed that my efforts to practice integrity and loyalty were worthy.

No company I knew proactively fostered the client's best interest over profit. Most of the industry emphasized sales or income numbers. This lack of a foundation of sincere service motivated me to establish my own real estate company. I was determined to treat everyone well, including my competitors. At a minimum, if I could cover my expenses and save for retirement, I knew I would be happy. I also did some pro bono work, which fueled my fire to help more struggling people. However, this volunteer work wasn't where my drive for genuineness—sincerely helping people—originated.

FIND YOUR ORIGIN STORY

Many define *success* as having wealth, status, and luxuries. I believe the best definition is being honest and trustworthy, *which is of value to those around me.* Throughout my forty-year career I have endeavored to be the Realtor with whom agents desire to work by focusing on thorough property research, high ethical practices, and generously sharing professional advice. Some agents told me they wanted their clients to buy my listings just so they could work with me. They drafted offers with prices and terms attractive to my clients that naturally maximized my clients' profits. Clients can financially benefit from their Realtor's good reputation.

An agent I once worked with was perplexed about how to advise her client on financing his purchase. Despite the agent, who appeared to be on the verge of a nervous breakdown, repeating the problem to me—"He can't do it. I'm a hot mess!"—I patiently explained the calculations of her client's down-payment requirements for different appraisal scenarios. I did this analysis for her even though it wasn't my responsibility.

"I know what makes you different. It's your genuine kindness," the agent said after realizing her client could finance the purchase, and she calmed down.

There it was again, the word *genuine*. While some have used the word to describe me, *genuine* is not a word I use in my personal vocabulary, so it made me wonder, "Since I'm unaware of it, maybe genuineness is my natural character."

Yet it wasn't until a Realtor surprised me with her comments at a recent industry event that I started to seriously think of where my narrative of success began. "I had to meet you because you won so many Aloha 'Aina [client service] Awards. I know how tough it is to win!" This longtime Realtor explained her understanding of the difficulty of winning this award. "My clients have been submitting nominations for me. I won once." Then she spoke about her observation of integrity as the exception rather than the rule. "I've been telling my agents to do the right thing for decades, but they don't listen to me."

A friend I saw at the beginning of the same event told me about the opportunity to write a story for a new book, *Mindset Matters*, with Jack Canfield. I waved my hand *no* and said, "I don't have anything to share." But the encounter with the "I had to meet you"

Realtor began to change my mind: "Maybe I do have something to share."

This self-examination sent me in search of my origin story. I could see the result of my choices: Some agents asked about my business secrets, which resulted in multiple awards, and a couple of real estate firms invited me to speak about above-and-beyond service. I needed to understand *why* and *how* I was different.

Over the years, some people told me they looked forward to reading the nominations my clients wrote about me, anticipating me winning. I reviewed my nominations, looking for mindset patterns. The following is an excerpt from a nomination:

> Though we only received one extremely low offer in six months from the previous listing agent, Suzanne suggested we list the property at a *higher* price. She fanned the flames of competition for the unit, resulting in a bidding situation, and ended with a value of $122,000 more than the other agent produced. We accepted an all-cash offer and closed in 2.5 weeks. It was spectacular!
>
> When buyers asked her to represent them, she remained loyal to us alone.
>
> Her *respect for her fellow Realtor wowed us just as much as our profit*. When Suzanne listed our property, she told us she would share some of her commissions with the previous agent to recognize that Realtor's effort. We told her it wasn't necessary. But she insisted. By the way, Suzanne doesn't know the previous agent other than acknowledging that agent as someone in the same industry. What Realtor suggests that another Realtor have the first opportunity to sell a property and then insists on sharing their commissions to recognize that the previous lister did some work even though there was a vivid performance contrast between the Realtors?
>
> We don't know of anyone else who gives to or respects their competitors as much as Suzanne does. She told us, "I want to be the Realtor whom other Realtors desire to work with." I know how Realtors are because I was a licensed

Hawaii real estate agent for fifteen years and own property in different states and countries. Suzanne stands out from the crowd in many ways, but mostly as the person whom EVERYONE desires to work with.

Aside from realizing why people labeled me "genuine," I had an epiphany of how I became this way—I inherited this quality from my grandmother, and it was the root of my striving to live a *genuine, generous, and grateful life.*

BE GENEROUS

My grandmother told me stories about how she and Grandpa were extremely poor. "You can't imagine. We didn't have anything! Absolutely nothing!" With an arranged marriage, they toiled side by side on their leased Hawai'i taro farm for decades. Grandpa delivered their eight children in the two-room hut he built beside their farm.

My mother said that after the Japanese bombed Pearl Harbor in 1941, military personnel came to search for signs of espionage in their home, and the men were shocked to find hardly anything there. The only valuables were their birth certificates stored in a coffee can. They didn't even have shoes or toothbrushes. Mom also shared her memory of Grandma sometimes not eating so Grandpa, she, and her siblings could.

Despite her meager background, Grandma showed me true wealth—to be generous, no matter the hardship. I saw her consistently give whatever she had, whatever was in her hand, to people she didn't know. And the recipients were surprised, then joyful.

I'm following Grandma's example of generous living—I freely give.

BE A CONDUIT FOR GOOD

In 2007 I heard Terry Parker, the National Christian Foundation (NCF) cofounder, speak about giving as a "heart issue." NCF exists to help people become wise, generous givers. Terry's speech stirred my heart, and for the first time in my life, I felt as if I had found my perfect fit—"This *joy of giving* is me!" I quickly established an NCF donor-advised giving fund and called it the Conduit Fund. I learned that wise giving is intentional, not casual, and I have been consistently donating to many Hawai'i nonprofits via my fund.

Another heart-stirring happened when I attended an exercise class held at Washington Middle School (WMS) in Honolulu. I grew up in this neighborhood and attended WMS. A man near the school entrance held a tin can and cardboard sign scribbled with "Going to mainland chess tournament. Raising funds." Five boys about age twelve stood beside him. I recalled reading an article about Washington's chess teams winning national tournaments. Most would have glossed over this article, but it jumped from the page and into my heart. WMS was a Title I school that received federal grants to help students in this low-income area. Despite this population's financial hardship, WMS produced students with skills superior to elite Hawai'i and mainland private school students. Immediately, I recognized this man and the boys as the coach and team about whom I had read.

I stuffed all the money from my wallet, about twenty dollars, into the can. Five pairs of bulging eyes darted over the can in awe that someone had donated what they thought was a generous amount. "Wow! Awesome!" they jubilantly shouted. Their reaction and recalling *my family's can* ignited my desire to help as many like them as possible.

The next day, I met with the principal and agreed to subsidize their travel expenses. This meant the coach could now field the strongest team with students who could not afford the trip.

One after the other, each team member won their match. Eventually, they swept the national tournament in Florida. During the competition their coach texted me photos and results as they occurred. I felt as if they were my children, and I cheered them on, whooping and hollering as any proud momma would.

Spurred on by this inspirational coach, the kids' grit, and

learning of other hardworking but needy students, in 2015 I established an annual Live Aloha Award. This award program incentivizes students to practice *daily* kindness toward others and develop the character to succeed. The school administration selects ten winners based on their projects in any mode of self-expression they wish, about how they or those they know live aloha. Among the six hundred students who attend the school, each of the ten winners receives cash, a personalized trophy and certificate, and recognition in front of the student body. This award is expanding into more schools.

How would you apply genuineness, generosity, and gratefulness to your life?

Consider What Drives You

Ask yourself, "What qualities do I strive to have? Can I authentically live those qualities to carry me through a successful career and the life outcome I dream of? Do I need to adjust my focus?" If so, write and implement daily habits and guidelines to help you achieve your goal.

Also, consider: "How have my experiences influenced my approach to work and life? What negative or positive experiences have been an impetus for my choices? Have I experienced deep gratitude that can lead to freely giving?"

Identifying and developing your values can result in a legacy beyond your career. How do you hope others will describe you? Their observations—good and bad—can be catalysts of crafting a more fulfilling narrative of success.

If you diligently apply your answers to your life, I believe one day you'll hear that big bell ring, not from a wall but from your heart, loud and clear.

About Suzanne

A Lifetime of Giving, Living Authentically, and Expressing Gratitude

Meet Suzanne: She doesn't just live life; she orchestrates it with the finesse of a master conductor, infusing every action with generosity, authenticity, and boundless heart. For Suzanne, life's purpose is clear: to be a conduit for good, channeling her resources to uplift others and profoundly impact her community. Her dedication shines particularly bright in championing positive youth initiatives exemplified by her Live Aloha Award.

The Conduit Fund: In 2007 Suzanne founded the Conduit Fund—a beacon of hope and support for families throughout Hawai'i. With a mission to empower families toward self-sufficiency, the Conduit Fund has emerged as a lifeline, providing timely assistance to over fifty charities. From housing support to welfare needs, Suzanne's fund is a testament to her unwavering commitment to helping others transform their lives for good and thrive.

Real Estate Trailblazer: Suzanne's accolades in the real estate world speak volumes. A six-time recipient of the prestigious Aloha 'Aina Award from the Honolulu Board of REALTORS®, she's earned the moniker Michael Jordan of the Aloha 'Aina Award for her unparalleled dedication and service. Clients laud her as a "genius" for creating competitive environments for her listings, and liken her to a real estate sherpa, guiding them through challenges with unmatched expertise to success.

Community Champion: Suzanne's impact extends far beyond real estate. In 2021 she was honored as the inaugural recipient of the Honolulu Board of REALTORS® Good Neighbor Award—an accolade that celebrates her tireless efforts toward positive change in her community. From nurturing resilience in youths to spreading joy through kindness, Suzanne's influence knows no bounds.

Life Beyond Work: Suzanne's zest for life radiates brightly in retirement. Whether strumming her classical guitar, gracefully gliding across the dance floor, or hosting delightful tea parties, she savors every moment with infectious joy. Inspired by the fleeting beauty of a blooming flower, Suzanne cherishes her relationships and delights in spreading love through personalized floral designs and heartfelt gifts.

Connect with Suzanne: Overflowing with gratitude and wisdom, Suzanne invites you to join her journey. Connect with her at suzanne@ ConduitFund.org or www.ConduitFund.org, and follow her on X (formerly Twitter) @SuzanneNakano, where she shares insights and inspiration on living a grateful life. She is happy to oblige with speaking engagements to encourage, challenge, and help people release more generosity and joy.

CHAPTER 6

THROWING AWAY A WINNING LOTTERY TICKET AND CHANGING THE WORLD

By Trisha Bailey, PhD

As I watched the rain trail down my kitchen windows, I felt run-down. But in the never-ending grind of getting my PhD and running two companies, I always felt run-down.

On a whim, I'd signed up for an online workshop on getting unstuck in your business, and on that Friday afternoon, I found myself with a few rare moments of quiet and could join live. I was seeking the answer to a question that had been nagging me for months: How can I find joy in my business, which is doing incredibly well but sucking the life from me?

The more I listened to that workshop, the clearer the answer became. My business was *never* going to bring me joy. Why? I'd built a company that didn't align with my values.

An avid believer in specific, defined goals, I knew that company's sole purpose was to sell for a predetermined amount of money on December 31, 2026, at 1:00 p.m. I'd then use that money to fund my partner's retirement, to give myself enough to live on, and to support thousands of social entrepreneurs.

Even though I was doing things for the right reasons, I see now I was sacrificing my most cherished values: freedom and solitude. The business was in the federal contracting space and was a constant cycle of panic, chaos, and blame.

Shook by my revelation, I needed to clear my head. Going for a walk, I asked my spirit an often posed question: Can I keep doing this business? The answer came back as always: Yes.

Then I asked myself something I'd never dared. Is keeping this business what's best for me? The speed and clarity of my spirit's response shocked me: No.

As I thought this, I stepped onto a sidewalk and noticed a garbage bin. I immediately had an image of me holding a winning lottery ticket…and then ripping it up and throwing it away. I knew my business could be my financial ticket, but now I also knew the sacrifice wasn't worth it.

Over the next eight days, I received nine separate confirmations that it wasn't possible to do something solely for the money and keep your soul. After fifteen years grinding in business, I started asking the right question: Was there another way?

Once I removed myself from the business and made physical and emotional space in my life, things started aligning for the future I'd always wanted. Resources and solutions materialized. I glimpsed a life where I could do what I loved without sacrificing all of myself to the endeavor. I took responsibility for my life and embraced the idea that if I had created something, I could uncreate it too.

It wasn't easy, but making the decision to walk away from that revenue was the best thing I ever did, and it opened an avenue to live my dream life, to help effect real change in the world, and to have something left of myself at the end of each day.

What People *Really* Want

Money's easy to make if it's money you want. But with few exceptions, people don't want money. They want luxury and they want love and they want admiration.

—John Steinbeck, *East of Eden*

After twenty-plus years working with both the most financially successful and the most impoverished, I've discovered no truer words than those spoken by Lee, the dutiful, philosophical Chinese housekeeper in John Steinbeck's classic novel *East of Eden*.

Don't get me wrong, money's great. But what humans truly want is everything money affords us.

Depending on one's native language, the words might differ, but the sentiment remains. Whether through a lush Central American rainforest, across the dusty African planes, on the Arctic ice cap, or down the languid Mekong River in Southeast Asia, each of us roaming this planet seeks something money itself can't buy.

Not cars, new spouses, or even "success." It's what we hope to get from all this success.

Significance.

SEEING THE WORLD AND OPENING THE DOOR TO MY FUTURE

I grew up in a small farming town in Dover, Florida, in a family filled with love, support, and an unerring belief in education and a strong work ethic.

When I was sixteen, I experienced my first major turning point. For the first time, I sat down and set myself a goal. From a white iron daybed in my pink-walled room, I asked myself a question: If I could do anything, what would it be?

I started writing my answer, filling the entire front and half of the back of a sheet of lined paper. My list included skydiving, learning to surf, and scuba diving with sharks. I didn't realize it yet, but I'd set the trajectory of the next decade of my life.

One day, while sitting in a physics class, I suddenly decided I'd had enough education. It was time to live! I bought a backpack and a plane ticket and spent the next three months in the South Pacific.

After what turned into a decade of traveling alone, I was in my thirties when I took my first humanitarian trip. I went to China and finally learned about traveling for a purpose.

After several subsequent trips to Southeast Asia, I saw firsthand how people were using businesses to help their communities. I saw people doing incredible good with so few resources and so many hurdles (rainy seasons, poor connectivity, roving blackouts). I saw them hiring the most vulnerable—refugees and those in the deepest levels of poverty.

I realized I could help these entrepreneurs in their important, life-changing work and was inspired to complete my PhD on the impacts of social enterprise training on trainees. By August 2020 I began this work in a more formalized way.

Since then I've been helping people pursue the use of business to build a better world, and that's the fulfilling path I continue on today.

CHANGING THE WORLD IS FOR EVERYONE

The biggest, most important mindset shift is that improving this world is not reserved for the wealthy. So many opportunities exist to partner with social entrepreneurs—business owners using their enterprises to empower others to lift themselves out of poverty, trauma, and violence.

There's no greater experience than contributing to something bigger than yourself, and everyone should know these opportunities are available to anyone who wants them!

Shifting from giving to sharing to partnering

Although it's often easier to see in hindsight, many of us have achieved great things. The question is, What comes next? What will you do with all that success?

For many, the answer's giving, whether of time, talent, or treasure. Giving is important and absolutely has its place, but an ideological problem can be inherent in this act. It's a one-way transaction. When times are good, you choose to give something to someone. But when times get tight, you might make the choice to withhold. These feelings of scarcity and protection are common human tendencies.

By shifting to a sharing mindset, it's a more free-flowing idea. It's an exchange rather than a transaction. In this dynamic, money has energy and a frequency, the same as light bulbs or ocean waves. Sharing simply becomes exchanging that energy for something greater.

The next progression shift is partnering. This takes the connection and relationship even further because you now perceive a vested interest in that organization's long-term success.

I first felt this shift when working with Mr. S, a dear friend. I met Mr. S through the Business as Mission global network. He's also a technology start-up founder and an Avant-Garde Entrepreneur Academy graduate. He's called to serve the "brick kiln families," a minority Pakistani group who live as modern-day slaves. While supporting him, I didn't feel I was just giving him money. I wasn't even sharing it in an energetic exchange. We were truly partnering.

Mr. S had all the social capital, access to, and trust with the brick kiln families. He knew what they wanted and needed: sewing machines and the opportunity to make and to sell clothes in order to feed their families, no strings attached. He gave them tools and education about making and selling, as well as emotional support and encouragement. The brick kiln families could use the money generated however necessary to support their families. My role as a partner was to support and to empower Mr. S any way I could.

Social entrepreneurs sit at the intersection of profit and nonprofit.

> Give a man a fish and you feed him for a day. Teach him how to fish and you feed him for a lifetime.
>
> —LAO TZU

Social entrepreneurs occupy a space between charities and for-profit businesses. A charity gives fish; a for-profit business sells fish. Social entrepreneurs sell fish in order to have the resources to teach many how to fish themselves.

Every type of organization is important and has its place. It's not about one being better or more valid than another. It's also not just about wealth redistribution. According to the UN, between 1990 and 2015, a billion people were lifted out of poverty through job creation. Most of that came through small businesses of fewer than ten people. Those effects trickle through the local communities and economies, creating a more sustainable, comfortable, healthy lifestyle for many.

Passion matters.

When many near retirement, their mindset is retiring *from* something. Wanting to get away from that job or situation, they think the answer to purpose is something—anything—other than what they have.

But the people who find peace and fulfillment are often those retiring *to* something. They use the time and resources afforded to them to follow their passions.

The same is true of social entrepreneurs. With passion and a purpose-driven mindset, there's a why behind the effort. Passion is the color on a canvas. It gives meaning to all the spreadsheets, goals, and meetings. Operating with conviction makes it easier to persevere on those inevitably tough days.

Social entrepreneurs go by many labels (change makers, missional entrepreneurs, impact businesses, faith-driven entrepreneurs), but they all share a passion for humans. The faces of the people they're helping drive and motivate these unique purpose-driven business owners.

You can contribute.

Feeling trapped or hopeless isn't limited to one socioeconomic group. To anyone experiencing those feelings or struggling to identify their purpose, know there are innumerable amazing ventures happening right now. Even if it doesn't make the news, so much colossal good is being done in the world.

This young network of upcoming social entrepreneurs is truly the next great generation, diligently working toward the Sustainable Development Goals to end poverty. Through their businesses, they're providing the tools people need to lift themselves into dignity, safety, opportunity, and equality, and what they need most to succeed is education, empowerment, advice, emotional support, and the encouragement to persevere.

And that support doesn't require going on a mission trip or venturing into the heart of Africa. Without even leaving your house, there are so many ways—financial and otherwise—to partner with these ventures and to change the world. *You* can be part of a solution, making a tangible, significant difference in people's lives. There's a place for everyone, and someone right now needs your special gifts.

Supporting and empowering social entrepreneurs is one impactful way to harness purpose and peace and create lasting, multigenerational change.

The three levels of support

What would it be like to know you don't have to travel halfway around the world to make a difference? If you want to help social entrepreneurs change the world, consider these three levels of involvement.

Level 1

These are the things you're already doing or can easily incorporate, including patronizing social enterprises or impact businesses when you travel and shop, and educating yourself about social entrepreneurship. Consider checking out *A New Lens*, a podcast with Jeff Shafer.

Level 2

Look at the organizations you already support financially. Get involved *directly*. Consider volunteering your knowledge, skills, or expertise with an organization like Global Switchboard. As you work together, your service will simultaneously encourage them and enrich your experience.

Level 3

This is the most significant commitment and potentially requires the biggest behavioral shift. At this level you can consult with your financial professional about investing in impact enterprises. (Not many do. Be prepared for them to look at you like you have three heads!)

You could also sponsor a social entrepreneur for online or in-country training, giving them access to invaluable education, support, and motivation.

Engaging in this level of support, you make a difference to people like Caitlin, who serves refugees on the Thailand–Myanmar border. Or David, a Ugandan man who couldn't afford a computer, so he built one with components found in the local dump. Now he teaches kids with no formal education how to code and connects them with clients who need software created.

What would it mean to know you're not just giving to social entrepreneurs but having an expected multigenerational impact on at least twenty-five people, including trainees and those trainees' young and elderly dependents?

Your generosity to a social entrepreneur is "teaching a man to fish" in action. Instead of putting a bandage on a bullet wound, partnering addresses systemic poverty, trauma, and violence. And that opportunity is available to everyone!

Does that sound exciting? This is my life's work.

I wake every day knowing I'm living my legacy. If this lights a fire in your heart, as it did for me, know you have many options to get involved. These problems are too big for governments to address, but we can effect change. We get to be the change we wish to see in the world.

Consider this your call to action. A moment to pivot from passive support to active engagement. Imagine the possibilities when we, together, take a stand. Will you join me in this movement to empower and to uplift through social entrepreneurship?

Living Your Legacy

Removing myself from my successful business was one of the best—and most difficult—decisions I've ever made. Throwing away that lottery ticket and walking into the unknown felt over-whelming, but once I did, everything started lining up.

I shifted intentionally, moving toward my natural gifts and pur-pose. I got quiet and listened to the answers presenting themselves. By doing that, I got to start my dream work and live my dream life six years ahead of schedule. My only wish is that I'd started sooner.

Embrace what matters to you now. Follow your passions now. There's so much societal pressure to leave everything behind, but what if you took a different path? What if you lived *in* your legacy?

Life always brings challenging seasons, but if you're seeing your impact, feeling the difference you're making, and experiencing the joy you're bringing, your significance and legacy don't have to feel like nebulous ideas. You can start seeing them today!

About Trisha

From the strawberry fields of Dover, Florida, to the global stage of social entrepreneurship and humanitarian work, Trisha Bailey, PhD, has forged an exceptional path. With a bachelor's degree in food and resource economics and a master of agribusiness management from the University of Florida, complemented by a PhD in international business from Northcentral University, Trisha's academic achievements set the stage for an impressive career.

Starting her career journey in public service with the State Department in Seoul, Korea, she navigated through a series of entrepreneurial ventures, from wealth management to commercial and industrial construction to municipal and federal contract fulfillment. Trisha's passion for blending business acumen with social impact led her to the forefront of social enterprise advocacy, where she has become a celebrated figure.

Her work in over sixty nations has centered on supporting social entrepreneurs, using business to drive serious change, especially in poverty-stricken areas. As the founder of her namesake initiative, Trisha Bailey, PhD, consults, mentors, and connects a diverse array of social entrepreneurs to foster sustainable economic development through socially responsible businesses. Her influence extends through her featured appearances in *CEO Weekly*, *US Insider*, and *The Women's Journal*, along with segments on NBC and ABC affiliates. Trisha is a member of impactful networks such as Business as Mission (BAM) and Good Market, solidifying her role in the global social entrepreneurship community.

Recognition has followed her hard work, with awards such as the Ellis Island Medal of Honor and a place in the Delta Mu Delta Honor Society. Her research and active role in global discussions showcase her commitment to business as a tool for good, making her a leading voice in blending commerce with social progress.

Beyond her professional life, she is deeply committed to her community and faith. She shares her life and adventures with her husband, John, finding rejuvenation in travel, literature, and the serenity of the ocean. Trisha's ambition to address the United Nations on the potential of social enterprises to contribute to global economic-development goals reflects her vision for a world where business serves humanity's broader needs.

Trisha Bailey, PhD, embodies the spirit of innovation, compassion, and resilience, making her a beacon for aspiring social entrepreneurs and a testament to the power of integrating business prowess with a profound social mission.

To learn more, go to www.TrishaBaileyPhD.com or scan the QR code.

CHAPTER 7

RIPPED AWAY

How Loss Brought Incredible Abundance to My Life

By Zack Viscomi

L ater, after the licking flames were subdued and the charred, smoky smell cleared from our nostrils, my dad described how we managed to get out alive. An angel had visited him in the middle of the night, urging him to wake up.

Even though my dad wasn't known to be a light sleeper, he did wake up that night, and the first thing he saw was a ghostly orange glow. It took him a minute to realize what was happening. Our house was on fire.

I was only three, but I vividly remember my dad ripping me from my bed. My mom had grabbed my sister, sixteen months younger than me, and we rushed down the stairs toward the front door. As my dad threw me over his shoulder, my young, groggy mind couldn't make sense of anything that was happening. Intense warmth where it should have been the cold of night. The brightness all around when I knew it should be dark.

I jostled against my dad's shoulder with every hurried step down and out of the house, and I soon found myself in the back of a car with my younger sister, Rachel.

"Don't leave this car," we were told, the voices tight and strained. "And don't turn around."

My mom dashed off back into the house to call 911. (This was before the era of cell phones.) As she feverishly dialed, the windows blew out, and I immediately turned around to watch the chaos.

Framed in the back windshield, I saw my dad running from neighbor to neighbor, knocking on doors. I saw towering orange flames. Lights sporadically flicked on, filling windows as more neighbors woke. Even from inside the car, I felt the hot, panicked energy.

We ended up moving a town over to a small industrial city that used to be a transportation hub along the Delaware River. Its glory days had long passed, and my parents did what they could to give us a good life. Dad worked, and Mom stayed home with us while we were little. We relied on government assistance to get by, but I have a lot of fond memories of my early childhood.

However, I also remember how much they fought. They tried their best, but their marriage ended up suffering the same fate as our early home. The evening their marriage went up in flames, I was asleep, jolted awake as my mom burst upstairs and into my room.

"Grab your things," she said. "We're leaving."

Disoriented, uncertain, and scared, I was once again ripped from my bed, only this time by my mom. My sister and I found ourselves once more in the back seat of a car, being shuttled to my mom's friend's apartment. As I lay on an unfamiliar couch, the grown-ups put on *Willy Wonka and the Chocolate Factory*. I watched singing Oompa Loompas while tears rolled down my eight-year-old cheeks from the news of their marriage having turned to ash.

Then, mustering what courage I could, I made a decision. I wasn't going to let this affect me. I stopped crying and vowed not to let anything get to me. Ever. I didn't know it then, but this was the start of my rebellion and self-destruction. I was going to do what I wanted when I wanted, and no one was going to stop me.

Even as my mom remarried, I weathered the firestorms of his rage with the same disconnection and rebellion. As I got older, I constantly sought ways to find escape and to blunt the sharper edges of my reality. That routinely meant partying, drugs, and alcohol.

As I approached the end of high school, everyone was telling me I should go to college, so I briefly attended school in North Carolina. But it was all a kaleidoscope cycle of partying and going to class, and I eventually woke one morning to a realization: If I didn't make a change, this was going to be the rest of my life. I needed something steadying, so I signed up for the Marine Corps.

Before enlisting, all military hopefuls must take the standard Armed Services Vocational Aptitude Battery (ASVAB) test. The maximum score on the test is ninety-nine, so the Marine recruiter and I were both equally surprised when my score came back. Ninety-three.

After testing that high, for the first time in my life, I felt someone looking at me like I had potential. The recruiter told me I could do whatever I wanted, and my best course of action would be enlisting in the Marine Corps Reserve, using the GI Bill, and going back to school to get my degree. I don't know if this was because he wanted to fill a reservist quota or if he genuinely cared about my success, but I am glad he said it.

I joined a reserve unit out of Red Bank, New Jersey, Sixth Motor Transport Battalion, and went back to school to get a bachelor's degree in business administration with a concentration in sales and marketing.

One of my best friends from high school, Nienke, was attending college in Philadelphia too. She introduced me to Alli, my future wife, and set the course of my life in a much different direction. I subconsciously knew my self-destructive path wasn't conducive to a long-term, healthy relationship. Even though I'd joined the Marines, I never stopped numbing myself with drugs. (I simply devised ways to get around the regular drug tests.)

By 2007, I was activated to be deployed, and true to myself back then, I dismissed my growing feelings for Alli. I couldn't handle the attachment to her and then leave for war. I wasn't emotionally capable of handling that burden, so I ghosted her, pulled back, and decided to cut ties with her—even though my heart was telling me to do something different.

The night before our active-duty orders went into effect, I did what I did best when I couldn't process my emotions. I celebrated my looming departure at a party.

God's plans are always bigger than ours, and although it didn't seem like it in the moment, my self-destructive, carefree life was about to unravel. Having passed several drug tests before, I wasn't worried when my name was one of only four called. It seemed everyone knew what was happening except me. I had finally failed a drug test.

I later found out I was only four points over the allowable limit of THC—just barely enough to constitute a failed test. To this day, I do not remember whether I smoked that night, but I owned up to it. In hindsight, I was really owning up to all the times I hadn't been caught.

For the first time, I faced the consequences of my actions and the possibility of being dishonorably discharged from the military. All things considered, I was a good marine and had received top marks. So, for whatever reason, they didn't kick me out. But they ripped my rank away, as well as my deployment. After the going-away parties and cakes and goodbye hugs and telling all my friends and family I'd be leaving, now I had to say none of that was happening because of a stupid mistake.

As I came to realize, though, everything happens for a reason. Still being on active duty, I had time to reflect on my choices and this gift of a second chance I had been given. I walked along the Jersey shore and asked God for help. I was ready to change my life, and it had to start by mending one bridge I had burned.

I had little courage at that time, so with a little help from a couple of adult beverages, I took responsibility for ghosting Alli. I also admitted my affection for her had never ceased. If she would take me, I wanted her to be mine.

She agreed to date me on one stipulation: I had to go to church with her. One hour of my time a week to date this amazing girl? "I'm getting the best deal here," I thought. Done! Going to church with Alli was the first time I heard the Gospel, and again my life was set on a different path.

It's often hard to see the progressive but compounding changes you go through, but I knew many people before and after becoming a Christian. Before, they were just marine buddies. After, many of them started coming to me with their problems. They wanted my advice because they trusted my opinion. They found wisdom in my thinking. As I reflected on that eight-year-old who set himself on a steadfast path of self-destruction and denial, this leadership role felt rewarding but surprising.

Shortly after getting married in 2009, I did end up getting deployed, and it cemented how much I enjoyed helping people. When I returned, I wanted to become a pastor, thinking that was my path. I received my master of divinity from Reformed Theological Seminary in 2015. However, I was not emotionally mature enough yet and in no way ready for the role. I still had a lot more work to do on myself.

Today, my journey of self-discovery has given me a greater perspective on my past and on my desired future. Vocationally, I have found my passion helping and coaching entrepreneurs to use their stories to connect with their audience and stand out from their competition. I'm fortunate and honored to work deeply every day with stories and mindset. After denying the impact of story for so long, it's inspiring and motivating to share with others how transformative harnessing that power can be!

FROM SELF-DESTRUCTION TO SELF-DISCOVERY

I spent most of my life not liking myself or my story. My life was structured around never letting anyone know the real me or what was going on. Everything was about winning approval and gaining people's acceptance, and that often meant ignoring my pain and living a reactive life.

Once I finally took responsibility and embraced my story, I could take these traumatic moments of being ripped away from all I knew and twist that narrative. I was no longer a bystander to my own story. I wasn't just reacting to what came my way. Now I was consciously and intentionally ripping apart the constructs of myself to the outside world, tearing away pieces of everything I wasn't dealing with.

I learned you often find the biggest value in the least-expected places. I never would have thought the thing that caused my self-destructive trajectory would also be the road map to getting healthy and well.

Looking back, after emerging on the other side, I could pinpoint a few key milestones that helped me embrace my story and use that to change my life and positively impact the lives of those around me.

It's why I started talking about the StoryMindset. The StoryMindset is all about understanding how story impacts your day-to-day life. The story you've lived. The internal stories you tell yourself. The stories others tell you. How all these combine either to propel you forward or to hold you back.

Here are some steps you can take to start working on your StoryMindset:

Recognize you have a mindset.

Even if you don't consciously realize it, you have a mindset, and it's affecting how you live and approach your life. While you might not think about mindset in those terms, it's worth recognizing that an open mind opens doors.

Rigid things tend to have a breaking point. Try to create a mindset flexible enough to withstand change over time. Bruce Lee calls this "being like water."

Take inventory of the language you use.

In the moment, be aware of what you're telling yourself. Start paying close attention to what you're saying and how you're saying it.

If you find yourself thinking you're not even going to try something because you've never been good at it, take inventory of that.

Be cognizant of those moments when your self-talk could be keeping you from success.

Figure out your values.

Shifting your mindset in a productive way requires your deciding what you want. What are your core values? What's most important to you?

The initial phase of shifting away from a self-doubt mindset is realizing this shift is necessary. It's a monumental and important step, but it doesn't bring about real change until the next phase: knowing what you want and crafting a life that's designed to go after that.

So many people operate without any thought around mindset. They're just surviving from moment to moment—until that system doesn't work anymore. When that happens, they're forced to examine their internal life and make changes.

If you look thoughtfully before you have to, that's a great position to be in!

Become the author of your own story.

From the stories we tell ourselves that keep us from the next levels of success to other people's stories about us, stories define our lives.

The right mindset is a way to become the author of your blank pages.

It's a way to look at your past not as a victim but as an empowered individual. When you embrace that StoryMindset and become the author of your life, you can see those past episodes simply as chapters in your story. They stop being able to dictate what you can and can't do moving forward, and they start becoming the foundation for the strong, resilient, intentional person you've become today.

You Are Your Story, and You Get to Write It

I was able to deconstruct and reconstruct a different life for myself by the grace of God, the undying patience and support of my wife, and a mindset shift. The StoryMindset is the path I took to embrace my own story and then use that to achieve greater levels of success—rather than run from it and destroy myself and those around me.

In business and in life, I believe steadfastly in the idea that your story is your key differentiator. No matter what that story is to date, it's what made you who you are today, and when you think about it in that way, it becomes a tool to help you achieve the life you want while also helping others.

For many years, I was ashamed of my story. I thought it was my weakness, but I found profound strength when I accepted that my story is part of who I am. It made the person standing in front of the mirror, and it made me the kind of person who wants to help other people.

It doesn't matter if you're trying to grow a business or achieve some other goal. The StoryMindset helps you recognize where you've been, where you are today, and how you can use that to become the most authentic and powerful version of yourself.

About Zack

Zack is an innovative leader, and his ideas are at the cutting edge of personal branding. He has helped hundreds of clients stay relevant, beat out their competition, and become the go-to authority in their field by building trust and credibility through media, marketing, and PR.

—JACK CANFIELD

Zack's journey began with a bachelor's degree in sales and marketing, which laid the foundation for his passion for and understanding of storytelling, strategic messaging, and brand management. Building upon this knowledge, he pursued a master of divinity, further refining his communication skills and gaining a deep appreciation for the power of storytelling and connecting with audiences on a deep and practical level.

During his eight years of dedicated service in the Marine Corps Reserve, Zack exemplified unwavering commitment and resilience. As a Combat Veteran, he gained invaluable experiences that honed his ability to adapt in high-pressure environments, make critical decisions under stress, and forge strong bonds within teams. These invaluable skills seamlessly translated into his professional endeavors, where he has consistently demonstrated exceptional leadership capabilities.

Currently serving as the director of brand development for Celebrity Branding Agency, Zack harnesses his expertise to craft compelling brand strategies that captivate audiences and elevate clients' brand presence. Leveraging his deep understanding of consumer psychology as it relates to story and storytelling, he guides clients through the process of defining their brand identity, creating impactful messaging, and leveraging that into strategic marketing campaigns.

He is a multiple-time best-selling author, and his work has been featured in *USA Today*, *The Wall Street Journal*, and *Forbes* magazine. He has also been seen on ABC, NBC, CBS, and Fox affiliates around the country. As an Ambassador for the Global Entrepreneurship initiative, he presented on the importance of story for businesses on stage at Carnegie Hall in New York City. He is also the host of the successful podcast for entrepreneurs *Elevate & Accelerate*, discussing the importance of elevating your brand to accelerate your journey to success.

Zack is passionate about helping people succeed while becoming the best versions of themselves. He also enjoys mountain biking and spending time with his wife, Alli, and their three children, Scout, Aries, and Poppy—not to forget their two dogs: a boxer-ridgeback-pit bull mix named Miley and a mini pug named Mona.

CHAPTER 8

LIVING YOUR PERSONAL LEGEND

By Mike Dusi

YOU NEVER KNOW WHO YOU ARE... UNTIL YOU HAVE TO

From animated hellos to loud, heartfelt laughs that filled every corner of my parents' pizzeria, I was a loudmouth—to put it mildly. A loyal customer entered my parents' restaurant and immediately stopped in his tracks. There I was, uncharacteristically eating a pizza with a fork and knife; I was frozen stiff. This customer was accustomed to my larger-than-life daily greetings, so for me to be seated still, not moving a muscle, meant there was something wrong... very, very wrong. Approaching me cautiously, the customer observed my frozen, twelve-year-old demeanor and noticed a tear rolling down my cheek.

In a whisper, he asked, "Mikey, what's happening? Are you being robbed? Are your parents OK? You're scaring me."

The truth was, I couldn't even feel the tear down my face because a few days earlier, I had woken up with my superpower gone. The one thing I treasured most in life as a twelve-year-old had vanished in an instant. My mother always told me, "As long as you smile, you can achieve anything you want in life." Now, however, my ability to smile was gone. Half of my face was paralyzed due to Bell's palsy. "MY LIFE IS OVER," I thought. Time stretched on agonizingly—first minutes, then hours, then days, and eventually months. I adapted by taking small bites, sipping drinks through a straw, and taping my eyes—which could not close on their own—in order to sleep. I was grappling with my new life.

One morning I woke up and momentarily forgot about the tape I had placed on my eyes the night before. In a panic, reminiscent of a Jim Belushi movie, I started flailing and screaming at the top of my lungs. "I'M BLIND! I'M BLIND! OH MY GOD, I'M FREAKIN' BLIND!" Overwhelmed by fear, I cried uncontrollably. It wasn't until I reached to touch my face that I felt the tape over my eyelids. Quickly, I ripped it off, relief washing over me.

Whether it was inspiration or desperation, this was the moment of a sharp, pivotal shift in my perspective—a transformation and reprogramming of mindset from broken self-pity to remarkable humility and gratitude. I was so appreciative of the fact I wasn't blind that I forgot how much it sucked to only have half a face. Here I was, instantly grateful for the half I did have! This realization sparked a powerful thought: If my mindset was beautiful, then so was I.

I embraced the idea that I, rather than external events, had control over my mind. Understanding that "energy flows where awareness goes," I discovered a new inner strength: overcoming any obstacle by simply being aware of what I was grateful for. From there, I adopted a belief in the boundlessness of my mind's capabilities, acting as if there was truly no limit to what I could achieve.

Gradually, I began to rediscover my former enthusiastic self, turning the predicament of having half a frozen face into a source of unparalleled comedy gold. If anyone thought I was a character before, they hadn't seen anything yet! I started having fun with the silliness of a frozen face, and—before I knew it—one morning I awoke to find the sensation in my eyes and cheeks returning. It was a miracle. It was as if I had been given a second chance to reclaim my original superpower.

However, my recovery brought with it far more than just the return of sensation to my face. It instilled in me a profound sense of gratitude for things I had previously taken for granted. As I came to reflect on my newfound change of perspective, I realized that my positive mindset did not just help me mentally; it played a crucial role in my face's physical healing as well.

The morning I was fully healed from Bell's palsy, I said my prayers and made a sacred vow to never allow anything—or anyone, including myself—to diminish my enthusiastic attitude and boundless energy for life. I came to understand that while I may not have complete control over the events that happen to me, I do have complete control over how I react in every situation. Bell's palsy represented the first significant challenge of my young life. By the grace of God, it didn't break me. Rather, it fortified me, making me stronger than ever before.

While most quantify success in the business world with money and money alone, I came to realize that mindset, specifically, was not about money or stature. It was about shaping myself into the respected and successful person I was destined to become. It was a process of leveraging the power of my beliefs—the most potent forces at my disposal.

My personal pledge soon grew into my life's mission, one of ensuring that everyone be left better after engaging with me than before I met them. I applied this to business endeavors, friendships, family interactions, and casual errands. From meaningful conversations to simple gestures such as a heartfelt "Good morning," a warm smile, or a friendly wave, I dedicated myself to looking for the good in people and making a positive impact. I was bettering the lives of those around me while simultaneously achieving my quest for purpose. Through this endeavor, what initially appeared as a setback transformed into a purposeful mission.

CHOOSE A LIFE'S PURPOSE WORTH YOUR LIFE

Eventually, I left New York. I wanted a bigger life than what Queens had to offer, and I jet-set to Los Angeles. When I arrived, I was a bull in a world full of yogis.

Soon I found myself dating a beautiful, outgoing model who

introduced me to a world of affluence. When her parents visited, they whisked us off in a luxury SUV to a Beverly Hills dinner, followed by a weekend getaway at the Deepak Chopra Center. My then girlfriend's family was incredibly wealthy, beyond the impressive real estate level. Think private jets, yachts, and an array of luxury possessions. On that first adventure aboard their private family jet, impressively piloted by the father, I secured the middle seat just behind the cockpit and experienced the thrill of takeoff firsthand. It was an amazing first experience!

While traveling, the mother gave me *The Alchemist* by Paulo Coelho, a choice that left me bewildered. I wasn't a reader, nor did I look like one. Still, I took the book. "If this is what super rich people carry around," I said, "I'll take it. Maybe it'll rub off on me!"

Months later, as we prepared to visit the family for Christmas, I heard the mother was eager to hear my thoughts on *The Alchemist*. At the very last moment, I dug it up and began reading. To my surprise, I absolutely loved it! It reminded me of the old Albanian folklores my father used to tell my brothers and me when we were kids.

An unforgettable moment came when, after narrowly escaping a horse's attempt to dismount me while I was riding on their snow-covered property in New Mexico, I went inside to warm up and ended up discussing the book with the kind lady who gifted it to me.

We touched on the thematic concept of "destiny as our only obligation." That fed into the idea of "wanting something so strongly, the whole universe conspires for us to get it." And then there was the handling of fear. "If we don't fear anything, we enjoy everything." And lastly, "the possibility of having a dream come true is what makes life worth living."

This conversation reset my mindset, reshaped my outlook, and reprogrammed my brain for the next stage of life. A valuable lesson for my curious self, it was an eye-opening affirmation of the transformative power of books.

The Alchemist affirmed my belief that learning comes from action, which dispels fear. Emphasizing impactful actions as true intelligence, life's journey teaches us everything necessary. Commitment to my path, trusting my gut instincts, and approaching everything with unlimited enthusiasm were key to shaping my personal legend. It wasn't just about external success but also about overcoming challenges and achieving profound personal growth, which carried the keys to forging a legacy beyond myself.

Taking risks and pursuing something meaningful is not just a recipe for happiness; rather, it is a requirement for a life truly lived. We do not fulfill a destiny by striving for daily comforts. We fulfill a destiny by believing we have unlimited potential and abilities—if you believe it to be true, the world will have no choice but to give you what you demand of it.

Initially skeptical, I now appreciate the genius behind the gift of *The Alchemist*. The woman who gave it to me recognized my potential and profoundly influenced my life's direction. I'm eternally thankful for her sharing her personal legend with me.

As the incredibly tough-minded Viktor Frankl said:

> What man actually needs is not a tensionless state but rather the striving and struggling for some goal worthy of him. What he needs is not the discharge of tension at any cost, but the call of a potential meaning waiting to be fulfilled by him.

SUCCESSFUL PEOPLE DON'T FALL ON TOP OF A MOUNTAIN

In the years to come, I found myself collaborating with incredible mentors and partners, leading the charge on several multimillion-dollar production deals featuring A-list actors in Hollywood. I embarked on a journey creating feature films across the US and abroad, navigating both domestic and global financial markets. My work paved the way to prestigious red-carpet appearances at every major film festival around the world. In doing so, I was crafting my very own hero's journey, embarking on an adventure that was both exhilarating and profoundly fulfilling.

One thing that took me quite a while to discover was the concept of "the obstacle is the way." Once I landed on this idea, however, it unveiled a tactical life hack. Books by experts who've navigated challenges and achieved success contain wisdom that can transform lives. Utilizing their insights, rather than relying solely on trial and error, enables us to access collective knowledge, shortening our learning curve and streamlining our path to success. Harry Truman famously said, "Not all readers are leaders, but all leaders are readers—they have to be."

Speaking of books, if you were to enter my office, you would notice a stack of them on my desk. Audiobooks play through my ears each day without fail. I devour everything from ancient scriptures to new publications. I typically have a one-year road map of what's awaiting me, and I always have my Socrates declaration whispering in my ear: "I know that I know nothing."

As I was growing up, my father's stories and fables, such as "The Path," shaped my family's morality and worldview. My brother Jack and I were so inspired by these stories that we collaborated with award-winning filmmakers around the world to bring "The Path" to life. We produced and filmed the project on location near our father's birthplace of Kosovo. In the film a young man's impulsive actions nearly lead to ruin, until an encounter with a wise old man changes his course. This interaction, highlighting the power of knowledge and reflection, turns a potential tragedy into a story of growth and unity.

If you take anything from this chapter, remember one thing: Go read. Learn from those wiser and more successful than you, and absorb their wisdom and experiences for your own personal growth. As Seneca said, "There is nothing more foolish than refusing to learn."

EVERY DAY, STAND GUARD AT THE DOOR OF YOUR MIND

A powerful tool I practice is my Sacred Focus Process. In this process there are four key quadrants: Family, Health, Business, and the fourth—a terrifying place that could cost you everything—The Devil's Vortex. And yes, the name should scare you. It is a category of life that includes all the distracting, energy-sucking, instant gratification-giving, and purpose-veering potential obligations, commitments, and plans that life has to offer. And it is a category with which you need to be *extremely* careful. Some people lose their lives in The Devil's Vortex. The goal, therefore, is to give as much of your energy to the first three, positive quadrants, known as the Holy Trinity.

By organizing all your thoughts and plans on paper, you can avoid falling into the trap of The Devil's Vortex and create a tangible process that truly clears the mind, ensuring your focus remains on tasks that genuinely matter. The more prepared you are, the more positive your attitude will be. A powerful tool I utilize is that of synchronicity, which states, "Self-discipline translates into habits, habits translate into consistency, consistency translates into speed, and speed translates into results."

As author James Clear says, "You do not rise to the level of your goals. You fall to the level of your systems."

Adopting this mindset is not simple. Designing my time for a daily commitment of reading, doing, and being present is a challenging yet extremely rewarding process. As leaders, we must embrace the fact we are the *lead characters* not only in our own lives but in our families' lives. It is crucial to take responsibility for that role with absolute dedication and pride!

I used to have vision boards, but now I have a physical board. On my desk I have "the shelf of knowledge," a tabletop of talismans and figurines that I have systematized into my own tactical mindset hack. Each piece on that desk represents a piece of the puzzle to my learned philosophies, strategies, tactics, and principles. The pieces are a direct window into and constant reminder of the core components that shape my decision-making processes across all areas of life.

Thinking, planning, and knowledge are cute, but those are only *potential powers*. Power only becomes *real power* when organized into definite plans of action and directed into definitive results. Whatever gets measured gets accomplished, so—on the flip side—whatever is not measurable must be made measurable.

Be the leader others seek. Embrace this motto: "Make no small plans." Make plans like an adult, but believe in them like a child. Only big, daring dreams draw attention—if they don't scare you, they're not big enough.

My hope is that you set goals so big that you cannot achieve all of them in your lifetime. I hope that you dream expansively and pursue those dreams relentlessly. Limitations live only in our minds, and when we master our imaginations, our possibilities become absolutely limitless.

As harped on ad nauseam by my mentor Dan Pena, "Man's greatest burden in life is unfulfilled potential."

I wish for you to avoid this fate. Rather, I hope your path is one of gratitude, perseverance, wisdom, and a purposeful destiny of your own making.

Pursue your personal legend, my fellow dreamers.

"When all is said and done...you gotta put in the work!"

About Mike

Entrepreneur | Real Estate Investor | Film Producer | Business Thought Leader | Best-Selling Author | Mentor

Mike Dusi is an entrepreneur, a film producer, a real estate investor, and a best-selling author renowned for his innovative approaches to both personal growth and professional advancement. Mike has spent the last twenty-plus years advocating and practicing the power of forward-thinking mental frameworks to transform aspirations into tangible realities.

In a career characterized by versatility, Mike has made significant contributions within the film, real estate, and business sectors. With a keen eye for the creative process and an adept hand at navigating the many facets and complexities of a film project's moving pieces, Mike has overseen productions in over six countries and nine US states, encompassing everything from high-budget feature films to commercials and music videos. His expertise includes domestic and international development, financing, preproduction, physical production, and postproduction, as well as distribution scaling theatrical to digital. His knowledge base has earned him widespread respect from his many peers, clients, partners, and audiences. Though much of this tenure stems from strategic agility, it is all a by-product of challenging the status quo of the mind, a theme deeply explored in *Mindset Matters*.

Beyond his successful career in film, Mike has carved an equally impressive niche as a distinguished real estate investor, where he excels in revitalizing distressed multiunit properties and single-family homes.

Whether on a film set, navigating the housing industry, or in the boardroom, Mike believes the key to creating better business and community futures is through instilling positive impacts in everything we do.

An elite keynote conversationalist, distinguished TEDx guest speaker, and televised interviewee across multiple continents, Mike strives to keep a firm pulse on industry evolutions and stay ahead of the curve in an ever-evolving world. He believes learning is something that is never finished.

A native New Yorker with Kosovar Albanian roots, Mike has always embraced his rich heritage. Having spent his formative years in the bustling borough of Queens, he traded the cityscapes of New York for the sunny vibes of California in 2003. Now soaking up the sun and enjoying the Cali lifestyle, he cherishes every moment with his wife and children in Los Angeles—where he strives to strengthen the foundations of his mindset with every passing day.

— Learn more at www.mikedusi.com —

CHAPTER 9

DEATH CAME KNOCKING, BUT GOD NEVER LET ME ANSWER

By Renetta Cheston

've escaped or eluded death more times than I can count. The first dodge was before I was even born. A coat hanger should have ended the pregnancy, but even after just a few short months in this world I was tenacious. I survived.

Several months after that my mom was watching *Blacula*, the blaxploitation horror classic. When she jumped at a particularly frightening part, she started to bleed everywhere and was rushed to the emergency room. The doctors told her it was time to have the baby, but it was about four months before my intended arrival.

When I did come, I was impossibly small, fitting neatly in the palm of a hand. The doctors solemnly declared, masks in hand, that I wouldn't make it through the night.

At the hospital at the same time were several members of the Shriners. Learning I had been born that night and that I wasn't supposed to see the next day, they ended up covering my medical needs during my hospital stay.

Despite the harrowing circumstances around my birth and all the evidence suggesting a different fate, I lived. Again. I had some lingering health issues from my traumatic birth, and the Masons took care of my medical needs until I was four years old.

Life was relatively calm during this time. My sister arrived two years after me, and my brother came two years after that. Then my parents separated when I was five, and everything changed.

As my father was walking out the door, he told me to take care of my brother and sister. At those words my young mind reeled. How was I supposed to do that? I was still such a child myself.

Before long our double-wide trailer devolved into a den of drinking, drugs, and partying. It was a revolving door of strangers, friends, and extended family.

The first time I was molested, I was six. Not long after, the same man cornered me in a back room and raped me. This initiated a decade of hell on earth.

For ten years there wasn't a day that went by when some man or woman in that house didn't touch me. Hearing my dad's words ringing in my ears, I felt it was my responsibility to save my brother and sister from that fate. So I'd routinely throw my young body in front of them, making a physical barrier between my siblings and the assailants. Sacrificing myself in the hopes they could escape that house unscathed and untouched.

When I turned ten, I finally decided to ignore the constant refrain not to breathe a word of what was happening to me. Before the service I confided in a preacher at my local church, telling him everything that was happening and that I needed help.

He told me he would pray for me, and after the service he took me into the private preacher's area.

"Whatever you hear in there," he told all the church mothers, "don't worry. I'm praying for her and casting a devil out of her."

He shut the door and assaulted me. No matter how loudly I screamed or what I pled, nobody came through that door to help.

Throughout this time, I was also being physically abused. Burned with irons. Beaten with broomsticks, metal, or anything available. Suffocated to the point of seeing popping stars of light behind my eyelids. I once had a knife to my throat, and I remember feeling nothing but relief. I was so impossibly tired. I'd switched off all emotions and walked through my existence like a zombie, letting whatever was going to happen to me happen. I invited the end, but it didn't come. Again.

When I was eleven, one assaulter tried to slit my wrists, but the skin proved too tough. I lived. Again. Today, all over my body I still carry the scars of deep lacerations from switches.

When I was seventeen, I ended up signing up for the military. I went into basic training, advanced individual training (AIT), and then the reserves. I wanted to go active and was sent to Fort Hood, Texas.

Before I could even get my bearings, I was lined up in a room with all my fellow reserves, and we all received a series of vaccinations. Even as we were shuttled onto a plane, we were told nothing. I looked around me and saw many people crying. Eventually everyone realized we were on our way to Desert Storm.

I served as an armorer, maintaining and repairing the weaponry. It was also my job to watch the eyes of the soldiers around me, vigilantly scanning to see when someone had checked out.

Death was around every corner in the Gulf War, but I was never taken. I was eighteen and nineteen years old, and I had to deal with the reality that fifty of our team went overseas and only twenty-five were coming back.

Several times my name was added to a mission, but then come the actual day, my name would suddenly be removed from the list and another put in my place. I remember sitting in Camp Victory, watching the vehicle carrying the team get smaller as it drove into the distance, and then hearing a deafening boom. Everyone gone in an instant. And I was supposed to be there, but I wasn't. Saved again.

Many years later, after returning to civilian life, death still seemed to stalk at my heels. In 2017 I was diagnosed with stage III breast cancer. Again, a roomful of solemn doctors delivered the bad news: six months to live. At that point, I wasn't even surprised when I beat it. I chose a natural way instead of traditional medicine, and the cancer subsided. On March 31, 2018, I was given a clean bill of health.

It is truly a miracle I'm here today, and I know only one thing could have saved me time and time again. Gave me breath through my first touch-and-go night in that hospital. Kept that knife pressed against my throat or wrist from ending it all. Years later, locked the steering wheel when I tried to drive into the median and jammed the gun I placed against my teeth.

The grace, mercy, and benevolence of God. He knew I had more to accomplish on this planet. He knew my story wasn't over and I had more gifts to give. It couldn't be the end because I was just getting started.

God's Greatest Gift of All

After a lifetime of being chased by death, God has showed me how to live. He's given me incomparable comfort, sending me miracles to get through the traumas. Helping me understand that darkness can never survive in the presence of laughter and humor. Revealing that I am not my past or anything that happened to me. Leading me to these most precious gifts—the critical mindset shifts that opened up endless possibility in my life.

Stay in the Word of God.

No matter what happens in your life, trust in the Word and truth of God. That will help you transform your mindset and give you the resilience you need to find your way with grace, humor, and light.

You are not what others say about you.

Growing up in a relentless cycle of sexual, physical, and emotional abuse in my formative years, I was constantly made to believe I wasn't enough. I wasn't smart enough. Good enough. Pretty enough. Worthy enough for love.

When you're told the same lie over and over again, especially as a child, it becomes programmed into the way you think about yourself, your abilities, and life. I've worked hard to deprogram myself from those hurtful, limiting labels imposed on me.

I'm becoming who God says I am, and so far I'm loving the answer.

When love isn't at the table, pack your bags and leave.

When you're faced with a situation that does not serve your highest and best good, it's OK to walk away from it. You don't have to fight. Just grab what you have and leave.

You deserve to be loved, cherished, and valued. If people violate that right, you don't owe them your time or attention. If someone in your life doesn't want to change, walk away. People can talk all they want, but until they show you change with action, you don't have to carry that person—not through life and not in your heart. You have incredible things to accomplish. You don't have time for people who refuse to change!

The hardest thing I ever did was walk away from my family, but when God said to go, I got up and left. If you're uncertain, listen to your intuition. If you're quiet, it will tell you when it's time to delete people from your life.

When I walked away, I started over fresh with God. I didn't know my next steps, but I kept walking and trusting God and the process. Was it scary? Yes! So much so. But I know God has given me the perseverance and strength to go on this journey.

If I can do it, anyone can do it.

I shouldn't be standing here today. I shouldn't be alive, and I shouldn't be whole. But I was able to emerge on the other side of all my trauma. I'm still here living, learning, and laughing.

If I can overcome and find the joy and unspeakable beauty in this world, anyone can.

When it's too much to bear on your own, God holds you up.

What I've been through is too much for one person to carry. As I spent time alone and got to know myself, I started remembering details of my past and tearing away at my story. The more I thought about it, the more I asked the same questions: How did I walk away with a pure heart? How am I still standing?

The answer is God. I couldn't do all of that on my own.

When your burden feels too heavy to carry, get in the presence of God. Sing songs. Read the Bible. That's when aha moments start to happen. God is in your heart, and you can access him whenever you need.

Keep your heart clear enough to hear when your intuition is speaking. It will keep you safe.

It's only by God's grace that I'm still here. If it wasn't for me changing my perspective and mindset and seeing things God's way, I know I would be dead or a lost soul.

It took every ounce of everything I had inside to make it out, and I know the real MVP is God. Without him I couldn't have done any of it.

To anyone struggling, remember that God is not just the God of salvation; He's also the God of deliverance and peace.

People who know themselves are unstoppable.

No matter what life throws at you, be your authentic and original self. Once you know yourself, the path in front of you becomes clear.

Changing your mindset is the hardest thing in the world, but it can be done. And once you do it, you become the dazzling, powerful, unstoppable force you are!

Change doesn't happen overnight.

I can't erase decades of abuse, betrayal, and trauma with the wave of my hand. Even after intensive work, I'm still getting to know who I am. I'm still nervous every day about this journey I'm on.

But I know I have God beside me, and that gives me the strength to tell myself I can do this. I give myself a pep talk every day, and then I keep going. Every day, I take small steps, and I know all that slow, incremental progress is carrying me toward my goals.

LEADING OTHERS TO THE LIVES GOD PLANNED FOR THEM

After everything I went through, my mission became helping others through dark periods in their lives. I opened a nonprofit aimed at helping women get back on their feet after loss, trauma, or pain. I'm a licensed massage therapist (LMT), holistic practitioner, life coach, and public speaker.

I'm also ministering to many different people, doing my best to bring as many lost, hopeless souls into the light and joy of life and the Lord as possible. I'm constantly working to help others change or remove the limiting, hurtful labels imposed on them by others and replace them with the labels God wants us each to bear.

Loved. Worthy. Enough.

About Renetta

Renetta Cheston is not just the author of *In the Garden with the Father: Understanding True Intimacy*, but a beacon of resilience and empowerment in her own right. A lifetime member of the Worldwide Women's Association, Renetta's journey is a testament to the power of faith, courage, and unwavering determination.

As a mother, grandmother, and jack-of-all-trades, Renetta recently experienced life-altering events that prompted her to seize the opportunity for a fresh start. Despite the challenges, she embraced the chance to rewrite her story, pursuing her dreams with relentless fervor.

Previously thriving as a licensed massage therapist and holistic practitioner in Atlanta, Georgia, Renetta's life took a sudden turn, forcing her to pivot and embark on a new chapter. It has been a daunting journey marked by uncertainty, but Renetta approached it with resilience and a steadfast belief in God.

Renetta advocates for others to take control of their lives and transform them, one mindset at a time. Drawing from her own experiences of ups and downs, she inspires through her blogs, demonstrating that restarting life is possible with hard work and determination.

A serial entrepreneur fighting for her freedom, Renetta is committed to living life on her own terms. Through her journey of self-discovery she has uncovered her true, authentic self and encourages others to do the same. Renetta believes that life is meant to be lived authentically, free from the constraints of societal expectations.

Her dream is to make a global impact by organizing nonprofits across various locations, spanning cities, states, and countries. Additionally, she is dedicated to supporting women who may have lost their path along the way.

Renetta Cheston's story is one of resilience, faith, and the power of embracing change. With unwavering determination and trust in God, she continues to inspire others to take control of their lives and pursue their dreams with courage and conviction.

CHAPTER 10

TURNING PAIN INTO POWER

*How an Unexpected Divorce Put Me
on the Path to Self-Fulfillment*

By Stacie Shifflett

I was the one who asked for the divorce, and believe me, I never thought that was even a remote possibility at that point in my life. I thought my marriage was the best it had ever been. What a stark realization that nothing could have been further from the truth.

Needless to say, my life was thrown into chaos. I ticked the necessary things off my list quickly. Hiring an attorney. Finding a home. What fueled me through that process was anger, which can be a powerful motivator, combined with a fervent desire to regain some stability in my life. From the outside, I had it capably under control. But on the inside, anger and resentment consumed me.

As I worked through the pain and trauma of my divorce, I frequently reminded myself of other tragedies I had overcome in life, such as the death of my first child. I had a mantra: "If I can get through that, I can get through this." Surely, I thought, my life will naturally evolve into its next chapter. To my surprise, though, it did not. I could not shake the remaining anger and resentment brewing inside me. It was exhausting.

That anger also stood as a barrier to future happiness as I felt victimized by my situation. This victim mindset shackled me to my past and blinded me to the possibilities of moving forward. Eventually I learned a stark truth. Liberation from the victim mindset is essential for embracing a new life chapter. This idea propelled me to dive fully into the world of personal development, marking the beginning of a transformative journey toward reclaiming my power.

I have achieved many things in life, each milestone a testament to the power of self-directed effort, determination, and mindset.

Without the traditional path of a college degree to guide me, I carved my own route to success. From mastering the complex world of technology to negotiating a fifty-million-dollar company acquisition with no upfront cash, my journey underscores that knowledge gained through experience and a relentless pursuit of goals can rival any formal education. Each accomplishment was a building block, laid by my own hands, in the architecture of my life.

From an early age the seeds of self-actualization took root within me. I harbored a strong belief in my ability to navigate life on my terms, often bending the rules to explore and to learn through direct experience. Raised in a Christian household, I questioned the use of religious beliefs as behavioral leverage. My youthful defiance was evident when I declared at a very young age, hand on my hip, "As long as I'm at peace with whatever I'm doing, I'll be OK." I cannot imagine the look on my mom's face hearing that from her five-year-old!

Now, many years later and after a lifetime of learning and experience, I have come to believe peace of mind is one of our greatest assets. It's the golden ticket to a fulfilled, purposeful life, but the prerequisite to internal peace is gaining knowledge. You have to step beyond what you know—or more accurately what you *think* you know—and expand your perspective.

I used this principle often in my life but never so dramatically as when I successfully acquired a fifty-million-dollar company...without investing one penny of my own money. I did this without an MBA or any other fancy college degree. I did this as someone who actually quit college to continue being a bartender and server.

When I married in 1983, I knew the hours I was working weren't conducive to married life, so I set about finding an office job. I did not have any experience, but my mother's church friend gave me an opportunity to work for her doing some administrative tasks, such as bookkeeping and word processing. I took to technology like a duck to water, and within a year I rolled out the first desktop computers to the entire US Department of Health and Human Services. I created and delivered all the operating system and application training and provided software support to the entire agency. Not bad for someone with no formal training!

Throughout my various careers I certainly benefitted from some amazing mentors, but I also had confidence I could do anything I put my mind to. And I did.

I became a sought-after subject matter expert in the field of federal government procurement. I wrote countless proposals that won many multimillion-dollar government contracts. I implemented complex procurement automation systems and integrated those systems with agencywide financial-management systems. This included reengineering business processes that aligned with the technologies. I owned a construction company for a decade. I even had a llama farm for years, raising award-winning llamas that I showed and sold throughout the United States. Honestly, there was a time in my life you could find me sitting in a board meeting in the morning and mucking out stalls in the evening!

I even had one of the world's top consulting companies recruit me quite hard to come to work for them. When I told them point-blank I wasn't interested, as I would not fit within their corporate culture, they created a position for me that allowed me to live life on my terms! *They* chose to "fit" into *my* world.

This is the power of mindset at work. I'm not afraid to think outside the box. In fact, I defy being put inside a box. I've always intuitively known you have to ask for what you want and put in the effort to achieve it—or you simply won't get it.

After navigating through a myriad of professional landscapes and personal trials, each chapter of my life not only fortified my belief in the power of a self-made path but also planted the seeds for what was to become my most fulfilling endeavor yet.

Despite my external success, an internal voice whispered about untapped potential and unexplored avenues. During a period of introspection, wrestling with the mindset that I was too old to embark on a new venture or that it was time to retire, I found clarity. The same resilience and self-belief that propelled me through earlier challenges now illuminated a new path forward. This wasn't just about defying societal expectations about age or career trajectory; it was about honoring a deeper calling—a call to serve.

Embracing this mindset shift marked the genesis of Modern Consciousness®. It became clear that my journey—replete with its highs and lows and hard-learned lessons—was not solely my own to keep. The real power lay in sharing these insights and in lever- aging my experiences to empower others to navigate their paths with greater awareness, purpose, and fulfillment. Thus, driven by a renewed sense of mission and calling on decades of acquired wisdom, I set out to create not just another company but a move- ment—a platform from which to advocate for the transformative impact of mindset.

From Discovering Myself to Sharing My Learnings

Honestly and meaningfully evaluating your inner world is never easy, but I stand here as an example of everything there is to gain from it. It is possible to reclaim your balance, joy, and peace of mind, and so much of that journey comes down to awareness, proper mindset, and aligned effort.

Throughout my journey, from personal trials to professional achievements, the following insights have been instrumental in shaping who I am, and they represent some of the profound wisdom I share with others today.

Fully evaluate all aspects of your current life.

In our lives we regularly monitor and evaluate so many things, from routine car maintenance and checkbook balancing to work performance reviews and annual physical checkups. But we generally assess these elements independently, in isolation from each other.

We seldom embrace a holistic approach to evaluating our lives, where every aspect is considered in its interconnectedness. The concept of a comprehensive life review remains largely untaught and overlooked.

In my Elevate Your Life® program, a life assessment is always the first step. Why? Because every journey needs a starting point to chart a course to the desired destination. When assessing our lives, it's important to focus not only on what's irritating or problematic but also on what's working really well. A life assessment provides the opportunity to see patterns and associations between areas of your life and allows you to reacquaint yourself with your character strengths, gifts, and beliefs. This is the foundation from which you can begin to get clear about the aspirations, goals, and outcomes you desire to create in your future. It seems daunting, but change rarely happens all at once. As Tony Robbins says, small shifts create big changes.

Nobody can change your life but you.

This can be difficult to hear, but it's true. After my divorce I was drinking, socializing, and traveling with friends. We were having a grand old time, and while it bridged a gap in my life, it wasn't a sustainable lifestyle for me. Who had the power to change that? Me.

I had learned this lesson once before when I lost my infant son. Trying to work through that hell, I went to exactly one group counseling session. I'll never forget sitting there and listening to a father talking about his loss five years prior. He spoke of his wife, who was still unable to leave the home, even to go to the grocery store.

Right then and there, I said to myself that I couldn't be that person. Even though I didn't have any answers, I knew I had to honor the grieving process and somehow move through this and continue living. If I remained victimized by the grief and tragedy of that situation, I realized I would never experience anything but grief and heartache.

Your life is your responsibility. End of story.

Break free from living on autopilot.

From birth we're programmed by our surroundings. Family, friends, and societal norms guide our every step, often without our conscious awareness. It persists as our lives unfold based on long-ago choices about relationships, careers, and personal paths. Sometimes life's unexpected twists jolt us awake, prompting a reevaluation of our default settings. Recognizing this, we face a pivotal opportunity. We are invited to step off life's treadmill and question whether our current direction truly aligns with our deepest desires and what we hold dear. It's a challenging but crucial step toward living in a way where each decision is a conscious choice aimed toward the future rather than a relic of your past.

Belief can make the impossible happen.

The power of belief is monumental. When I told people I wanted to acquire a multimillion-dollar tech company without any money, I was met with a great deal of skepticism and eye-rolling, as you can well imagine. Despite the doubts and challenges, my unwavering belief in the vision and my capabilities turned the so-called impossible into reality. This journey underscored a crucial lesson: With the right mindset, relentless faith in oneself, and what I call "right action," overcoming seemingly insurmountable obstacles is not just possible; it's achievable.

Lean in to divine timing.

Embracing divine timing means trusting that events unfold for a reason, though it might not be immediately clear.

When I cashed out of the tech company in 2010, I started my next company, Agility Construction, with insights and assistance from my then husband. Then our lives imploded. I used to say I never would have embarked on that venture had I foreseen the end of my marriage. Yet that sentiment belies the truth of the invaluable freedom and opportunities owning that company afforded me. Running my own business granted me the autonomy and resources necessary for a profound personal-development journey, including traveling the world as a Tony Robbins Platinum Partner for two years.

This experience taught me the importance of reframing our perspectives. The unexpected twists in our lives are not setbacks but precisely timed opportunities for growth, guiding us to where we need to be.

Learning never stops, and healing isn't linear.

Growth and healing are continuous journeys, not linear paths. Embracing intentional living means committing to constant practice and transforming desired mindsets into intrinsic parts of who you are.

Throughout my divorce I learned that healing demands facing our emotions head-on, not burying them. Initially, revisiting old wounds I thought I had dealt with was frustrating, but over time I learned to view these moments as opportunities for deeper understanding and growth, as they were presenting me with a deeper level of healing. Greeting these moments with open curiosity and a calm mind versus frustration marked a step toward becoming a newer, more evolved version of myself.

Understanding that growth is an ongoing cycle of learning, healing, and evolving helped me embrace each new phase in this journey of life with trust and calm.

Choose your words wisely.

The power of language cannot be overstated. It shapes our perceptions, influences our thoughts, and even alters our emotional landscape. In the midst of my divorce I believed I was experiencing anger, only to realize it was grief masquerading as rage. This revelation allowed me to embark on a genuine path of healing, accepting the past and moving forward with grace.

Reflecting on my marriage today, I see it not as a lost chapter but as a foundational part of my journey. It blessed me with the gift of my son and invaluable lessons learned. By reshaping the narrative in my mind, my divorce transformed from a source of anguish to a mere event in my life's tapestry, and I was able to release any lingering emotional burden.

This journey taught me the transformative power of self-talk and reframing our stories. It's a testament to the idea that our experiences, no matter how challenging, contribute to the fabric of who we become. Embracing this, I hold no desires to alter my past or to feel my time was wasted, for it sculpted me into who I am today, and for that, I am grateful.

USING MY WISDOM AND EXPERIENCE TO GUIDE OTHERS

My divorce set me on a path of personal development that I've been travelling since 2012. I have transformed the incredible grief, pain, and anger of that experience into wisdom and emerged from that experience stronger, more self-aware, and more keenly poised to help other women find their paths to success.

As a Modern Consciousness Coach®, I am able to use my own growth journey to help others rebuild their lives and reclaim that essential sense of joy and peace of mind.

This business is just one in a long line of reminders that everything happens for a reason, and I am able to do this rewarding, important work because of—not despite—my pain.

About Stacie

Founder and CEO of Modern Consciousness® LLC Entrepreneur | Modern Consciousness Coach® | International Best-Selling Author

Stacie Shifflett, founder of Modern Consciousness®, is a catalyst for personal transformation. With a diverse background in multiple industries, she has become a sought-after expert in empowering individuals to reclaim joy and peace of mind.

In 2012 a life-changing event propelled Stacie on a quest to better understand herself and the human condition in general. Her immersive exploration with experts in diverse fields of study ignited a deep desire to guide others toward embracing their unique brilliance and finding their joy.

As CEO of Modern Consciousness®, Stacie channels her insights to help individuals raise awareness of unconscious patterns from the past. By shifting these patterns intentionally, she enables clients to transform their lives from frustration to internal peace and joy. Stacie firmly believes that embracing Modern Consciousness® is the secret sauce to a life well-lived.

Stacie's credentials speak to her dedication and expertise. She is a multiple-time international best-selling author, a Modern Consciousness Coach®, a certified ThetaHealer®, a Free-mE® emotional freedom technique (EFT) practitioner, and a master practitioner of neurolinguistic programming. Her expertise extends to being a Professional Neuro-Shine Technology Coach™ and a Certified High-Performance Coach™.

With compassion and commitment, Stacie inspires personal growth and conscious living. Through her visionary leadership at Modern Consciousness® she empowers individuals worldwide to embrace their innate brilliance and experience authentic joy and peace.

- **Website**: www.ModernConsciousness.com
- **Facebook**: https://www.facebook.com/ModernConsciousness
- **Instagram**: https://www.instagram.com/modernconsciousness
- **LinkedIn**: https://www.linkedin.com/in/stacie-shifflett-7b5a8922
- **You may contact Stacie at** Empower@Aware.Life.

CHAPTER 11

MINDSET SHIFT FROM ROCK BOTTOM

By Leslie Randolph Braggs

"You don't escape trauma by ignoring it. You escape trauma by confronting it."
—ISABEL WILKERSON

ROCK BOTTOM

I don't think anyone would look forward to being taken away for inpatient psychiatric care, even if it was voluntary. I sure know I didn't. Looking at the young lady that was getting admitted along with me, I could see that she didn't either, as she rocked back and forth in her chair dressed in a blue outfit that resembled scrubs but was made of paper. I wondered, "What pushed her to her breaking point?" Then my gaze moved to the nurse sitting behind the window of the dimly lit space, a middle-aged, robust black woman in powder-blue scrubs who asked me in a slightly authoritative but caring voice, "Young lady, are you here due to the Baker Act?"

I didn't know what to say, but the attendant that had escorted me from the hospital bent down and whispered in my ear, "You are a voluntary admission." I felt a slight ease of the shame that coursed through my body for not having a clue of what she meant, as I answered in a timid voice, "No, ma'am."

I have always believed in the scripture Romans 8:28. In summary, it says that everything that happens to you will eventually work out for your good because you love God. I love the Lord, but it was hard to envision anything beneficial coming out of this situation. Crafting a new narrative was essential for my success, or at least my survival. I had to learn the lessons and put into action the changes that were required. At the time, I didn't realize that it would all begin with a shift in my mindset.

Entering a psychiatric facility strips away a person's sense of identity. After taking a trip to the emergency room, raging in response to my husband's outburst of anger, the medical staff strapped me onto a gurney and wheeled me away. My daughter, who had driven me to the hospital, frightened at what was happening, was told she couldn't escort me. After they check you in and determine you should be admitted, they take your possessions and clothing in exchange for paper blue clothes and those booties with the little rubber dots on the bottom so you don't slip and fall.

The people in a place like that might surprise you. Some seemed down on their luck. Others, like a high-profile lawyer that was there, easily resembled anyone you'd see in a downtown business meeting. You just never know.

Within the confines of the facility, a comforting sense of structure emerged as I settled in. Having served nearly three decades in the military, I knew what structured life and routine felt like. Yet the turbulence of my recent existence had cast structure aside. Now there was a time for everything—medications, meals, and bedtime.

Some people would struggle with a regimented routine like that, but for me it offered respite. Letting someone else worry about life's necessities allowed me time to think. To really feel things out. I knew right away that I wanted to get better and get out.

Outside of meds, meals, and bedtimes, we participated in activities that not only occupied our time in a positive way but gave us something to reflect on.

I remember being asked to draw a picture that showed how I was feeling. Without much thought I drew a young woman. She was wild and manic. Later I took her to another class where I had to describe the emotion she displayed. She looked exhausted. I empathized with her having reached her breaking point. That picture haunted me.

I had arrived at rock bottom! I knew that if I was going to get out of this, I had to change my ways and alter the mindset that got me here.

To do that, I had to get back in touch with who I was.

Twenty-Eight Years of Service

I was quite the people pleaser growing up. Somehow I instinctively knew how to identify and care for other people's needs. Sadly, I didn't learn what it meant to take care of myself.

Being the oldest of four girls, I recognized that my father wanted a son. I remember the day I overheard Daddy express that sentiment after the birth of my youngest sister. Even before the term *girl dad* was coined, he cherished being a father to daughters but had hoped for a son to carry on his namesake.

To make my dad happy, I vowed to become the son he didn't have. We went to football games. He taught me how to change a tire. We did many things that fathers do with their sons.

My father was my high school principal. In our state he rose to a prominent place in academics. Pleasing him also pushed me to excel academically, earning valedictorian in my high school class.

In other efforts to please my dad, I enrolled in the Reserve Officers' Training Corps (ROTC) while in college. Sometimes I like to joke that I joined because I liked green, or that the ROTC boys were cute, but deep down there was something much deeper there.

I was pretty good at getting along with men and was comfortable around them, particularly ones like my dad, older father figures who were well directed. I was a decent athlete, and since I had given up being a girly girl, a career in the Army seemed well suited for me.

Because I loved the fact that ROTC was filled with guys, I

sometimes appeared aloof in class. One of my academy instructors vowed to see that I never received a commission. I know this because he shared that with me many years later. Well, I showed him. I worked as hard as I could to become the number one cadet in my class and first female battalion commander in the school's history.

Twenty-eight long years later, that was just a small taste of the obstacles I faced, but also learned to overcome. The military taught me a lot. It made me the kind of fighter that can overcome anything.

When I look back, I'm proud of what I accomplished during those early chapters of my life. But part of the recognition about being a people pleaser came down to seeing some hard truths.

For all my efforts, my dad never told me I was beautiful. At least I don't ever remember hearing him say those words. He rarely said that he loved me either. His love language was "acts of service" meaning he showed love by doing, but his actions didn't translate into the words I needed to hear. As I got older, I began looking for validation from all the wrong sources, which resulted in years of unnecessary heartache and pain.

WALKING ON EGGSHELLS

I was drawn to my husband because of his striking looks and impressive talent. His stage presence and voice were something to behold. What I didn't realize was that behind his attractive appearance was a covert narcissist—a person who could seriously hurt others emotionally if not careful. This is not an official diagnosis, but he certainly displayed all the traits. Unfortunately for me, I didn't see it until it was almost too late.

My husband, on the surface, came across as charming. That's the word I use to describe his effect on people. Whenever he needed something, he turned on the charm. He could make you laugh too, which on a superficial level feels good.

But my husband's real skill was mirroring other people. He

behaved similarly to the people he was with, which made them feel special. Whether he was out on tour, playing shows, or meeting fans backstage, that kind of shallow connection went a long way.

In the music business, people are drawn in by humor and flattery. Between his dashing good looks, the breathtaking talent, and his charm, my husband opened many doors for us. I was living a celebrity lifestyle, which can sweep a girl off her feet or keep her head in the clouds.

Behind closed doors, when we were alone, things were different. Our seemingly deep connection quickly eroded. Early on in our marriage, I overlooked the red flags, due to his intoxicating love bombing campaign.

All my life I sought validation from a man like the man my husband pretended to be, so when I received it, on the surface it felt good. But there was a much darker side emerging. We were rarely intimate, that side of him was reserved for the public. For me, a rare PDA went a long way. While this man brought me so much joy, he inflicted twice as much pain. Then, little by little that pain became overwhelming, and the joy left altogether.

Everything in our marriage came crashing down when COVID shut the world down. Suddenly, instead of being out on tour, we were at home—together; at least we were physically. Those unmasked tendencies started to rear their ugly heads. Depression struck hard. Rather than open up, he avoided talking to me about anything meaningful. One minute he was ignoring me, and the next, when entertaining guests or out in public, his mood would lighten.

It was like the story of Dr. Jekyll and Mr. Hyde. I struggled with this cognitive dissonance. I had fallen in love with a man who seemed on the surface to be filled with life and charm. But that wasn't who he really was. My husband revealed himself as cold and uncaring; being with him started to take its toll on my body and mind.

THE BODY HOLDS THE SCORE

His effect was profound. In the beginning I gave him a pass, blaming his childhood wounds or thinking it was something I did.

But then I started getting sick. I had GI issues, which eventually resulted in me losing control over my bodily functions. I began experiencing chest pains, heart palpitations, and frightening panic attacks that came from out of nowhere, compounding long-buried traumas. A few times I ended up in the emergency room, struggling to get my body right again.

When I felt well enough, I went to church and prayed about things. I even convinced my husband to go with me to counseling.

Nothing I did worked, though. I was on a downward spiral. The woman who retired from the Army in great shape had gained weight and now found it difficult to breathe during normal activities.

Being in a marriage with someone whose mood shifted with the wind was stressful. Because of the control, constant gaslighting and manipulation, my identity was hijacked, and I no longer knew who I was or just how far I had fallen.

I came to the realization that my husband was not concerned with repairing the relationship he had seemingly worked covertly to destroy. Yet I continued to work hard to pay our bills and keep our household afloat, while he treated me like an unwanted roommate. I thought if I could love harder, mention my unmet needs less, and accept the disrespect of our vows, I could save our marriage. It was then I started to challenge my poverty mindset. I became accustomed to the crumbs of affection or kindness thrown my way. I was worth more than that contempt!

It took time and a lot of pain to finally see the truth. Reality became clearer when the man who was so against getting a pet made the offer, unknowingly inviting a spark of wisdom into my world.

A dog's love is unconditional. Each day when I came home to

my puppy, she was so happy to see me. I can't say that she saved my life, but I got a glimpse of what I was missing: being loved.

Then, about three months later, a dear friend I had deployed with to Iraq succumbed to brain cancer. This hurt deeply. We had become very close during our deployment. I considered him the little brother I never had, and he would lovingly call me "big sis."

At the wake his wife spoke. She told us that although her life would never be the same, she would be OK because she had been well loved. Those words haunted me because I realized that I had not been well loved but *well hurt*. As a wife, I had endured manipulation, lies, insults, and stonewalling; been denied intimacy; and been gaslit from the man that had promised to love and cherish me. Nevertheless, I strived each day to show unconditional love and extend forgiveness. I suffered silently, living the lie with him in public, while everyone else, including animals, were showered with respect, kindness, and humor.

When I returned from Matt's funeral, I had the grounds from which I could change my unhealthy mindset. My husband decided to leave.

After the Change

After drawing that exhausted young woman during my inpatient art class, I took a step back, inspired to draw another woman who confidently declared, "I can do this."

The contrast between them was profound. On one side stood a woman worn down, drained, and seemingly powerless. On the opposite end of the spectrum was someone poised to embark on the journey of self-transformation, ready to put in the work to bring about significant life changes.

While questioning the identity of these women, a realization unfolded—they were both me. Each represented different facets of a wounded self that had endured fractures for far too long. Recognizing this duality within myself, I understood that growth demanded a change from one version of myself to the next. I realized that achieving this hinged on a fundamental shift in mindset.

I used to say that I needed to marry somebody like me to take care of me. It was a joke, intended to be funny. But there was also an element of truth in it.

For most of my life I have sought external sources for fulfillment. I constantly looked to others for validation, believing that love from someone else confirmed my worth. In retrospect this perspective was flawed. Pinning my hopes on being a daddy's girl or striving to please a man who refused to embrace me for who I truly am proved to be a misguided approach.

I realized that the key to self-fulfillment wasn't found in external relationships but within myself and how God viewed me. A shift in mindset occurred as I turned inward, recognizing the need to love and forgive myself. I discovered that the true source of strength lay in acknowledging my own beauty and embracing the inherent power within me to effect change in the world. What my mind envisions, my body can accomplish. Indeed, the essence of transformation lies in the profound impact of one's mindset because your mindset truly matters.

About Leslie

With a distinguished career spanning over twenty-seven years on active duty in the United States Army, Lt. Col. (ret.) Leslie Randolph-Moss (her official name while serving) has lived a life filled with experiences that many can scarcely imagine. Her roles have been varied and impactful, ranging from administrator for military hospitals to company-level commander, officer career manager, investigator, and medical advisor to the Army Inspector General at the Pentagon, not to mention serving as a physician assistant and medical director for acute-care clinics. Leslie's tenure included combat tours in Iraq and East Africa, embodying a spirit of service and sacrifice.

Beyond her military achievements, Leslie is the author of *The Great Imposter*, a literary work that chronicles her deployment experiences, showcasing her adept storytelling. Her endeavors extend into founding Infinite Love Redemption, a brand dedicated to empowering women and young girls to navigate the uncertainties in their quest for purpose. This mission is deeply personal for Leslie, a survivor of sexual, physical, and emotional abuse. Her life's work is to illuminate the path from victimhood to victory, assuring women that thriving post-abuse is not only possible but paramount.

Leslie's talents and commitments run deep. An accomplished musician, she has written and recorded a worship CD, and as a transformational speaker, she is a beacon of hope and healing. Her affiliation with The John Maxwell Certified Team as a speaker/trainer/coach, as well as Lisa Nichols' Certified Transformational Trainer, alongside hosting a podcast, allows her to reach and inspire a broader audience. Leslie's dedication to women's rights, particularly in East Africa, where she aims to combat genital mutilation and support church-building efforts, underscores her global vision of empowerment and faith.

As the proud mother of three incredible adults and grandmother to two beautiful granddaughters, Leslie's personal life is as rich and fulfilling as her professional and philanthropic endeavors. Her anticipation for the release of her full literary work, stemming from the insights shared in her book chapter, is a testament to her ongoing journey of impact and transformation.

Leslie's story is one of overcoming, serving, and leading by example, a step toward changing the narrative of secrecy and shame surrounding abuse. It's an invitation to join her in crafting a new narrative for success, grounded in courage, transparency, and infinite love.

Currently Leslie resides in Jacksonville, Florida, where she works with a physical medicine group at Brooks Rehabilitative Hospital, Florida's number one rehab hospital, providing world-class interdisciplinary rehabilitative care.

Information on how to contact Leslie:

- **Instagram:** Instagram.com/infiniteloveredemption
- **Facebook:** Facebook.com/profile.php?id=61556166596275& mibextid=LQQJ4d
- **Email:** LesRandolph@infiniteloveredemption.org
- **Phone:** (904) 834-1339

CHAPTER 12

MATTERS OF THE MIND AND HEART

Paths to Restoring a Broken World with Love

By Julie Meates

What if the power to enhance or destroy ourselves, one another, and the world lies in something as straightforward as our mindset? Within the fabric of humanity lies the constant propensity to gravitate toward good or evil, flourishing or diminishing, growth or decline. We are not stagnant beings. Indeed, we gravitate toward the trajectory of our dominant thoughts.

What if the answer to right our wrongs in the pursuit of healing is love? The connection between mindset and heart forms the essence of love's profound expression. Our mindset serves as the fertile soil where the seeds of affection and empathy take root, intertwining with the tender fibers of the heart. It is through our mindset that we cultivate the capacity to perceive love's nuances, to embrace its complexities, and to navigate its ebbs and flows with grace and understanding.

When the mind is attuned to compassion and positivity, the heart blossoms, radiating warmth and kindness to those around us. Conversely, a hardened mindset, steeped in negativity and fear, can cast shadows upon the heart, hindering its ability to love fully and unconditionally. Thus, the symbiotic relationship between mindset and heart is pivotal in nurturing love's transformative power, allowing it to flourish and illuminate even the darkest corners of the human experience.

In the midst of the chaos brought by consumerism, slavery, and genocide, a relic of World War II poses a question: Can love endure without the element of chance, or is it at risk of fading away amid fear, regret, and apocalyptic visions? Winston Churchill lauded the cracking of the German Enigma Code as pivotal in winning the war.[1] However, as contemporary conflicts and crises wreak havoc in lives, homes, and lands, we must ponder: Are we pursuing the right path? Or, as Al Gore said in 2006, "Is this *An Inconvenient Truth*?"

Is humanity's essence about unraveling the mysteries of love, revealing the nourishing fruits beneath its tough exterior? Or do we risk unleashing chaos akin to historical plagues and power struggles? Every individual stems from a family, despite its form, even in the face of tragedies like child soldiers and oppressive regimes. Yet nations like the US and NZ grapple with the highest incarceration rates, imprisoning not just bodies but minds and hearts. As some exploit the earth, others strive for change.

Which narrative will we embrace? Like the resolution in 2022 at the SuccessSummit in Beverly Hills to end slavery and human trafficking, will we dare to embrace change, seeking the true essence of love? Is this a World Vision?[2]

COMMON THREADS IN LOVE, BEAUTY, AND COMMITMENT

Imagine pledging to love, honor, cherish, and respect not only one another in marriage but extending these vows to encompass people, places, and the planet. Could such a broadened commitment make a tangible difference?

Marriage, an ancient pact dating back millennia to Mesopotamia, was forged to fortify family bonds and alliances. Some marriages flourish amid abundance, love, joy, shared land, and resources. As Jack Canfield aptly notes, "Your inner guidance system is your joy," guiding you along life's path.[3]

Consider Akaroa (a Maori name that means "long harbor"), a town on the Banks Peninsula, southeast of Christchurch, New

Zealand. This haven of beauty where dawn brings forth blooming pohutukawa and cheerful birdsong, a radiant vista of love and joy on the horizon. Yet amid such beauty, what sustains enduring marriages while others falter into grief and disaster?

This chapter unveils both sides of the coin. Despite hardships, humanity's beauty can shine through, even amid genocide and calamity, akin to a resilient aster flower blooming in adversity. What if conflicts, whether at home, at work, or across the globe, share a common thread, perpetuating the very problems we strive to solve? Such discord breeds confusion and deep disconnection, akin to a sinking ship with an enigmatic code engulfed by fear and suffering, as Vanzant poignantly portrays in *One Day My Soul Just Opened Up*.

WHEN PEOPLE ARE TOXIC

Far too common and familiar is the epidemic of toxicity in our broken humanity. The collateral damage influences our everyday lives and exists all around us. When surrounded by nurturing people, we can grow healthy and caring. However, negative and toxic influences can make you feel as if you're in a constant anxiety-inducing war zone, even within your own mind, causing harm, whether physical or emotional, even gaslighting.

According to statistics from the National Domestic Violence Hotline, more than twelve million women and men in the United States suffer from rape, domestic violence, or stalking by intimate partners each year, eroding their self-esteem and perpetuating cycles of physical, emotional, and psychological abuse. Maintaining such relationships can be stressful and lead to heartbreak and low self-esteem. These statistics reflect a global issue: One world operates on greed and fear, and the other thrives on love and hope.

Imagine if, like all precious things, vows extended beyond their bonds to encompass people, places, and the planet. Could this broader commitment make a meaningful impact?

Marriage, akin to a paua shell, may seem hard on the outside, yet beneath lies a vibrant beauty shaped by life's currents. To sustain its splendor, it requires vigilant care, like regular maintenance checks and services ensuring smooth navigation along life's journey. It is a cherished jewel in life's crown, deserving of love, respect, and meticulous attention. The key lies in treating one another with tenderness and honor, recognizing that partners are not meant to be each other's rehabilitation centers.[4] As Billy Graham once aptly said, marriage does not have to be perfect to be great.[5]

In *The Prayer*, as sung by Andrea Bocelli and Celine Dion, the dream of enduring and fulfilling marriages is underscored by the importance of good communication and mutual respect, enabling partners to continue dreaming and singing together in harmony.[6] Several themes shine through this powerful piece:

With eyes to see and wisdom as they journey through life: a reminder to appreciate, affirm, show affection, apologize, seek forgiveness, strive for altruism, loving respectful attention, not addiction.

At times when unsure: a reminder not to blame. Don't judge; try to turn it around to the positive, showing compassion, caring, contentment, cooperation, consideration. Manners matter. Please and thank you.

The Prayer: a return to love. Love is patient and kind.[7] As the Dalai Lama reminds us, "Be kind whenever possible. It is always possible, and if you have to choose between being kind and being right, chose kind, and you will always be right." He assures that a sense of loving-kindness leads to greater calmness and happiness.

When uncertain: Steer clear of John Gottman's Four Horsemen of Relationship Apocalypse: criticism, including harsh startups; contempt; defensiveness, including denial; and stonewalling. Such negative behaviors spell disaster for any relationship.

Guide them: a reminder to encourage and lift others up through active listening, offering support and validation. Remember, during conflict keep up that 5:1 ratio of positive-to-negative interactions.

With grace guide each step of our journey—even if we step in the wrong direction and need forgiveness, reconciliation to foster harmony: End the day with gratitude. Seek to be at peace with others. "We don't go to sleep with some remaining differences between us," Jimmy Carter told the Associated Press in 2021.[8]

Keep us safe in arms of love: Remain in love. As Kahlil Gibran reminds us in his classic, *The Prophet*, "Love one another, make not a bond of love: Let it be a moving sea between the shores of your souls."

THE POWER OF CHOICE

Within each of us lies the pivotal choice between war and peace. What if a solution to inner war also solves the outer war? You might believe small actions hold little significance, but consider how a match ignites a fire, a minor hole leads to a leak, or a kink disrupts water flow. A golf ball can find glory in a hole in one or stray into the wilderness, just as a knot or a virus can unleash unforeseen consequences. A single bullet can end a life, while a needle can relieve a blister or mend a garment crafted with time and love. Thoughts, words, and actions hold weight; unresolved conflicts breed profound pain in our lives and world.

However, it is in the small, seemingly insignificant choices we make that we craft a new narrative for success, akin to the pillars of a happy marriage: honesty, unselfishness, spirituality, teamwork, and contentment.

The delicate interplay between the individual and the collective emerges as a poignant theme. What if our perception of self extends beyond us to embrace the interconnectedness of all beings and the universe itself? As we navigate the complexities of existence, we realize that every action, every thought, every word resonates beyond the confines of our immediate sphere, rippling through the fabric of reality like echoes in the cosmos. A simple act of kindness, a smile, a moment of empathy, a word of encouragement—these seemingly small gestures reverberate far beyond their initial manifestation, shaping the world in ways we may never fully comprehend. We are not solitary entities but integral threads in the intricate web of existence, each thread contributing to the vibrant mosaic of humanity and the universe.

With each step taken in this journey, we learn to navigate interpersonal interactions more adeptly, transforming moments that once spiraled into futile disputes into opportunities to manifest God's love. As we embrace this evolution, interactions fraught with irritation and discord become fertile ground for the emergence of profound connections infused with God's omnipresent love.

Inspiring Thoughts from Dalai Lama[9]

- "The more you are motivated by love, the more fearless and free your action will be."

- "Take into account that great love and great achievements involve great risk."

Dalai Lama also says the following regarding positive thinking:

- "A positive attitude is essential for one's physical and mental health."

- "The true hero is one who conquers his own anger and hatred."

The wisdom of the Dalai Lama underscores the profound significance of maintaining a positive outlook on life, recognizing its profound link to both mental attitude and physical well-being. Thus, it becomes imperative to consciously opt for positivity, thereby unlocking one's true potential. Drawing inspiration from the Dalai Lama's teachings, we can employ these pragmatic strategies to nurture a positive mindset and transcend negativity:

- **Embrace a solution-focused mindset:** Redirect your focus from dwelling on problems to exploring solutions, avoiding complaining, as it is draining. View challenges as avenues for personal growth and enlightenment.

- **Cultivate an attitude of gratitude:** Regularly acknowledge and celebrate the blessings in your life. Gratitude serves as a catalyst for fostering positivity and cultivating inner contentment.

- **Surround yourself with positivity:** Seek out the company of one another, literature, and activities that radiate positivity and inspire personal growth.

- **Embrace mindfulness:** Engage in mindfulness practices to anchor yourself in the present moment and heighten self-awareness. Mindfulness empowers you to consciously choose positive thoughts and attitudes, fostering a harmonious inner landscape.

MINDSET MATTERS TOWARD THE WORLD WE LIVE IN

Fostering positive relationships and cultivating harmony extends beyond our immediate circles and humanity to encompass our care for the environment and the world at large. Offering sincere appreciation for the natural world's beauty and resilience fosters a deeper connection and inspires stewardship. Actively listening to the concerns and needs of our environment without judgment allows us to understand its challenges and work toward sustainable solutions. Providing support through practical actions such as conservation efforts, sustainable practices, and advocacy reaffirms our commitment to preserving the planet for future generations. Just as Pope Francis emphasizes the importance of "May I?,"

"Thank you," and "I'm sorry" within the family unit, embracing these principles in our relationship with the environment promotes harmony, gratitude, and accountability, paving the way for a healthier and more sustainable world.

LEMA SHAMAMBA AND WOMEN OF HOPE FROM DRC

For the Women of Hope from the Democratic Republic of Congo, or DRC, the promise of enduring love is shattered. Like so many, Lema Shamamba suffered the violent loss of her husband at the hands of rebels. While many would succumb to bitterness amid such grief and the atrocities of rebel groups, Lema emerges as a beacon of hope, transforming profound loss into a voice of reason and optimism for her nation. As a refugee in a distant land, thousands of kilometers from her kin, she speaks locally and globally, yearning for the world to heed the cries of her war-torn country and envision peace in its verdant rainforests. Holy scripture emphasizes the interconnectedness of humanity, echoing the words of Jesus, "Truly I tell you, just as you did it to one of…these brothers and sisters of mine, you did it to me" (Matthew 25:40, NRSVUE).

The DRC grapples with severe repercussions, including Congolese refugees fleeing for survival and a brighter future, rampant poverty, and the unchecked exploitation of Congolese minerals. The devastating deforestation of the world's second-largest rainforest exacerbates climate change, robbing the planet of a crucial carbon sink. The social and psychological toll of these violations is immense—chronic fear, helplessness, and fractured communities plague the Congolese people. Persecution ravages lives and erodes fundamental beliefs, much like the rainforest's gradual decline as a vital carbon sink and the heart of our world. As Michael Beckwith suggests at Agape: "Get your ship together," why not regulate those who are trying to tear down the rainforest and create so much pollution?

An unseen digital war brews,[10] with devices surveilling[11] our moves and fake news fueling distrust, even cyberattacks and cyberbullying. Data centers and algorithms shape our behaviors. Meanwhile, the DRC's rainforest hemorrhages refugees for technology, fueling conflicts and slavery. The electronic industry profits despite the toll: seven million lives lost in conflicts over "conflict minerals," perpetuating slavery and genocide. According to the Global Slavery Index (2023), an estimated fifty million people are trapped in slavery globally. Electronics remained the highest-value at-risk product (US $243.6 billion).[12]

Lema Shamamba and the Women of Hope from the DRC bravely highlight the enduring suffering of Congolese women, from colonial rubber exploitation to modern conflicts over resources such as coltan, which is essential for technology in electric cars and smartphones. They advocate for hope amid despair, emphasizing the importance of restoring vibrancy to women's lives. Without hope, despair prevails.

Deforestation for resources such as coltan harms the environment and communities, disrupting habitats, exacerbating conflicts, and contributing to climate change. Urgent action is needed to protect Congo's ecosystems and mitigate the destructive impacts for future generations.

The sociopolitical upheavals of the twentieth and twenty-first centuries breed widespread persecution and human rights violations, including torture, mass killings, and home demolitions. How can we mend shattered lives and prevent further destruction?

Our mindset holds the key to addressing the challenges in our lives, communities, and world. Our daily decisions shape our world, whether supporting sustainable practices, advocating for social justice, or caring for our neighbor. Let's commit to cultivating a mindset rooted in empathy, compassion, and responsibility, recognizing the interconnectedness of all life and the urgent need for collective action. Let us rise to the challenge of reevaluating our attitudes and behaviors, for in doing so, we have the power to forge a brighter, more sustainable future for generations to come.

NOTES

1.   Hugh Sebag-Montefiore, *Enigma: The Battle for the Code* (London: Weidenfeld & Nicolson, 2018).

2.   "Open Letter: Progress Modern Slavery Legislation Before the Election," OurActionStation, accessed June 17, 2024, https://our.action station.org.nz/petitions/progress-modern-slavery-legislation-before-the-election?

3.   Jack Canfield, *The Success Principles* (New York: William Morrow Paperbacks, 2006)

4.   Matt Brown with Sarah Brown, *She Is Not Your Rehab: One Man's Journey to Healing and the Global Anti-Violence Movement He Inspired* (New Zealand: Penguin, 2021).

5.   Billy Graham in Alysse ElHage, "Billy Graham's Legacy Includes a Loving, Faithful Marriage," Institute for Family Studies, February 22, 2018, https://ifstudies.org/blog/billy-grahams-legacy-includes-a-loving-faithful-marriage.

6.   Andrea Bocelli and Celine Dion, "The Prayer," on These Are Special Times, Columbia Records, 1998, and Sogno, Philips, 1999.

7.   1 Corinthians 13:4-8.

8.   Bill Barrow, "Global Power Couple, Best Friends and Life Mates: Inside the Bond Between Rosalynn and Jimmy Carter," AP, updated November 26, 2023, https://apnews.com/article/rosalynn-carter-death-jimmy-relationship-0b3b3b6c4dcb462265253c8e98f70228.

9.   "Dalai Lama Quotes on Peace of Mind," Level SuperMind, accessed June 17, 2024, https://level.game/blogs/50-best-dalai-lama-quotes-on-peace-love-and-inner-strength?lang=en.

10.   Huib Modderkolk, There's a War Going On, but No One Can See It (London: Bloomsbury Publishing, 2022).

11.   Shoshana Zuboff, *The Age of Surveillance Capitalism: The Fight for a Human Future at the New Frontier of Power* (London: Profile Books, 2019).

12.   "The Global Slavery Index 2023," ReliefWeb, updated June 19, 2023, https://reliefweb.int/report/world/global-slavery-index-2023.

About Julie

Julie Meates is a New Zealand-born humanitarian with a diverse career, endeavoring to bring more peace, kindness, and love into the world. Family is central to her life; she is married with three children and a large extended family.

Beginning her career as a teacher, Julie's passion for education and health led her to become a qualified social worker and counselor. She is now a barrister and solicitor, actively pursuing post-graduate studies in education and health. Her commitment to community well-being is evident in her extensive volunteer work, driven by her paying kindness forward.

In 2002 Julie cofounded the Fulfil A Dream Foundation, with a vision, hope, and dream of strong and happy families; happy, healthy, vibrant communities; and wise and visionary leadership, uniting high-profile figures from all fields to empower individuals, families, and communities. She also was the chairperson of a Maori learning center (indigenous Kohanga Reo).

Julie is a seven-time best-selling author, coauthoring books including *Pay It Forward* with Brian Tracy, *Success, The Soul of Success, vol. 3, Turning Point*, and *The Keys to Authenticity* with Jack Canfield, along with *Never Give Up* with Dick Vitale and *Rise Up!* with Lisa Nichols. These books contribute to various causes, including nonprofits dedicated to ending human trafficking and modern-day slavery, among others.

Julie joined Abundance Studios as a producer and worked on notable films including *The Truth About Reading*; *Dickie V* documentary; *It's Happening Right Here*, which earned a Telly Award in 2023; *Tactical Empathy*; *Hero*; and *Conquer 100*. She has also been a guest on TV shows such as *Hollywood Live, Times Square Today*, and *The Global Entrepreneurship Initiative's Summer Symposium* at Carnegie Hall. Her appearances have been featured on NBC, ABC, CBS, and FOX nationwide.

Julie has volunteered with Community Law's programme, in community justice panels. The community justice process aims to repair harm caused by offenders promptly, using restorative justice processes. She also served as the board secretary for the United Nations executive in her Canterbury region and is involved with the Women of Hope Wake Up and Help Ourselves Trust Board.

Throughout her career Julie has volunteered with Women's Refuge;

various NGOs; charitable organizations; and sport, musical, cultural, social, and community lead initiatives, empowering youth, families, and communities. She held the position of vice president at Wairarapa International Communities Inc., engaged in community radio with local, national, and international broadcasts, and contributed to homelessness initiatives across the globe.

Julie Meates is a compassionate, kind, and inspiring leader, empowering diverse groups of people to achieve their goals.

CHAPTER 13

THE WOBBLY LADDER

By Gary Sprouse, MD

The courtroom was cold, and my feet echoed on the slick stone floors as we made our way to our seats. My future, my identity, my reputation—all hung in the balance. The events of the last two years had rocked my entire world. My marriage had fallen apart, my finances had taken a severe hit, my practice helping people in my community suffering from chronic pain had been taken away from me, and all...*for what*?

The judge cleared her throat, reviewing the documents in front of her. As we waited, I thought about how another me, a younger me, might have been taken to his knees under the stress. But here I stood, head high. Because I knew something my younger self didn't: I knew that all my patients were better off because of my care.

It was weeks earlier, sitting on my couch, watching the movie *Shrek*, when the thought first crossed my mind: "I might not be able to be a doctor anymore." I had already jumped through every hoop the medical board had assigned: the license suspension, the eighteen months of retraining with a pain-management specialist and psychiatrist. Still, it hadn't been enough.

In the rural community in Maryland where I practiced medicine, local doctors functioned as a kind of one-stop shop. We were family practice and urgent care all rolled into one. We provided some specialty care when no specialist services were locally available. I liked having that kind of contact with my patients, being able to bandage them up when they were hurt and advise them when they were well. It created a kind of trust that I've always known was necessary to successfully care for people.

From the moment I opened my practice, it was clear that there were a lot of people in my community suffering with chronic pain. Pain management was not yet a medical specialty at the time. Doctors were being encouraged to treat pain aggressively with the use of opioids.

Our edict was simple: prescribe enough pain medicine to treat a patient's symptoms while minimizing the side effects. Using this as my guiding light, I had helped dozens of people become pain-free and able to reengage fully in their lives. Even though opioids can have serious side effects, such as addiction, they are one of the best tools doctors have for pain management. But while I was practicing, the pendulum of public opinion on opioid use began to swing, and I, and many doctors in my position, got caught up in that swing—casualties of a shift in opinion.

Sitting there, watching Shrek's green-faced optimism, I realized I was going to need to get flexible. I was going to need to work hard and see myself out of this situation.

I was going to have to start practicing what I preached.

———•———

I don't know what had me reading so much that year. My wife at the time had told me I was stressed and needed to see someone about it. I mean, sure, I had stress in my life. I was running a busy family practice, I had young kids who needed a lot of my attention, and we were still in a phase of building our financial future. I was working hard, and there was little time for anything else, but wasn't that just this season of life? I dove into books. I had always been a reader, but this was something else. I devoured them. Books on neuroscience, on quantum physics, on chaos, and on productivity. I would disappear to our basement and read in whatever spare hours I could carve out.

The book that changed everything was called *The Structure of*

Scientific Revolutions, by Thomas S. Kuhn. In the book he argues that scientific advancement is not a straightforward evolution but rather a "series of peaceful interludes punctuated by intellectually violent revolutions," and that in those revolutions "one conceptual world view is replaced by another."

Meaning: paradigm shifts happen in an instant. I like to think of this like a wobbly ladder. You're climbing up, everything's going along fine, and then at some point things start to get a little shaky. For a while you fiddle with the steps, the feet, the braces. You try to adjust or reposition the ladder, but nothing works—because it turns out the problem isn't the ladder at all. The problem is the *platform* the ladder is standing on.

You must find an entirely new place to stand. That's a paradigm shift.

I had a paradigm shift in my basement, in the middle of the night, reading about scientific revolutions. I suddenly understood everything I didn't even know I had been trying to understand. I began to get a picture of how you get a *mind* from the human brain. I began to understand how letters become words and words become books and books become a shared human consciousness.

I wrote and wrote. This started the groundwork for my model of Strataspheres. Strataspheres is a tool that changes how you can perceive and process current information, and gain world-changing new insights (book forthcoming).

You might be asking yourself, "Who is this guy to develop a theory of, well, everything? I was asking myself that same question alone in the dark basement. I understood that I had stumbled onto something that could be life-changing for me, my family, my patients, the world, but I didn't know yet how I would (or could) implement it.

The truth is that people who come up with—or discover—paradigm shifts aren't usually people who are inundated in a particular industry. I was a generalist in every sense of the word. As a doctor practicing in a small underserved community, I had to know a little about just about everything to do with the human body. In my life as a curious person, a thinker, and a seeker, I had read and learned a little about a lot of subjects.

So perhaps I was *exactly* the person to start a paradigm shift.

To understand the idea of Strataspheres, imagine a picture of the earth cut in half so that you can see a cross section of all the layers within. Let's let this imaginary earth be a metaphor for human evolution, one layer, or sphere, to represent each step forward.

At the innermost layer is energy. Wrapping around that, atoms. Then molecules, inorganic material, organic material, living things, and, eventually, human beings. Each of these are layers in our cross section. At the outermost layer, we humans have added an entirely new layer because of our mind skills (more on that in a moment). Let's call that layer "choice," or "free will."

To transition from one layer to the next, two things must be true: there must be quantity (meaning more than one of any element) and interaction between those elements.

A single atom doesn't do much of anything. But take two hydrogen atoms and a single oxygen atom, and put them together? You get water. A completely new form, with emergent properties that you could never predict just by looking at hydrogen and oxygen.

That's how we get from one place to another. That's how we move between the spheres, and it's these jumps from one layer to the next, both in our personal lives and as a society, that give us growth and satisfaction. It's cooperation, not competition, that is the main driver of evolution. Can you imagine the difference in all of our lives if cooperation was our primary method of growth? The repercussions would be mind-boggling.

But (in a perfect illustration of the model itself) the theory of Strataspheres doesn't do much good to anyone without quantity (meaning people know and understand it) and interaction (meaning they value cooperation more than competition). So after my epiphany in the basement I spent months trying to figure out how to make my understanding mean something, viscerally, for the people around me.

I knew I had to find a way to utilize the insights of Strataspheres to do real-world good for my patients and community.

Like any great paradigm shift, after my long night in the basement I began to see the world differently, and what I started to see—particularly in my patients—was how the gifts of their minds were also the things most likely to get in their way.

As people, one of our greatest mind skills is the ability to envision a possible future. Lions don't have this. They don't sit around thinking about what their life is going to look like if they don't find enough gazelle to eat. They just see a gazelle and go after it. Win or lose. But as people, we know how to think forward. Sometimes decades into the future.

Now, a shaman or a guru might tell you just to *be present*. They might teach you that if you stop envisioning the future, you'll also stop worrying. That might be true, but why should we be forced to give up one of our greatest skills? The very thing that allowed us to jump from one sphere to the next in the first place!

Instead of giving up my greatest skill, why not just eliminate or at least reduce the side effect, *the worry*? In patient after patient, I would see this same pattern play out. They were ill or down on their luck, and the stress about their situation was making them sick, or sicker. But was it the stress about the situation? Maybe a situation is just a situation, and the stress comes from projecting onto it our fear about the future. It wasn't the illness robbing people of their happy place; it was the side effects of their thinking.

At the time I faced discipline from the medical board in Maryland, I was just one of many doctors facing similar tough questions. I saw colleagues fold under the pressure and willingly give up their medical licenses instead of having to suffer through the gauntlet of hearings and court cases and examinations. Had I not been fully enmeshed in my own work around happiness and stress, I might have been one of them. But because of my own understanding of the power of reaction, I knew three things to be true:

1. My identity, as much as it felt compromised, wasn't actually at stake. Yes, I was a doctor, but that's not all that I was. I was an investor, an author, a father, a karaoke singer. I was me, Gary Sprouse, and all that I contained.

2. If I were to spend my time only focused on the bad things that could happen, I would buckle under the stress. I had to adopt a stance of realistic optimism. I couldn't wear rose-colored glasses and pretend it was all going to be fine. I had to work hard so that I could survive, financially, and so that I wouldn't find myself in this situation ever again.

(I have a little saying, and it goes, "The harder I work, the luckier I get." It's never truer than when the chips are down.)

3. Even though the medical board was saying I was bad and the judge was saying I was bad, I knew that I was good. I knew that I had served my patients, that they were happy and healthy and had vouched for my abilities as a doctor. *I knew that I had made the best choices I could make with the information available to me at the time.*

Guilt is an interesting feeling because many of us have it even when there is no basis for it. Guilt is a by-product of doing something wrong, so when guilt bubbles up, you must ask yourself, "Did I do anything wrong? Is there evidence that I did something wrong?" In my case, there was no evidence. I had followed a reasonable standard of care, and all my patients were better off because of my care. So even when eventually my board took away my ability to prescribe controlled substances, I didn't let guilt grab hold of me.

Because I knew and understood these three things: who I was, how to carry on with less stress, and that I didn't deserve the emotion of guilt, I was able to remain flexible and see myself to the other side of an intensely challenging situation.

Because I was flexible, I was able to jump at opportunities as they presented themselves. I began investing in real estate, something I'd wanted to do for a long time. I found a new job practicing medicine at a nursing home, one that gave me a bump in salary and an overall reduction in stress. I was able to retire from my practice at an age that felt right for me and devote myself full time to writing and teaching.

Because I was using my skills without succumbing to the side effects, I was able to see that I was in the midst of a paradigm shift. The ladder beneath me had become dangerously shaky, and the only way out was to find a new place to stand.

You can't control what happens to you, but you can control how you react. You can also do the work to understand why and how you're reacting.

Again and again in my work I see people resigning themselves to living their lives stressed out because they don't see any other option. They believe their circumstances are the cause of their stress, and circumstances are a heck of a lot harder to change than mindset. Once you begin to see that your reactions are what cause stress—and that your reactions are completely in your control—the helpless feeling goes away.

You start to realize that not only are most stressful situations temporary, but it's possible to live in your happy place, no matter what is happening on the outside.

It's been many years since my epiphany in the basement, and I have been sharing my insights and tools for reducing stress ever since. I have spoken on numerous podcasts, have written and spoken on the subject for audiences large and small, and go deep into how to apply these tools to your own life in my book *Highway to Your Happy Place*. I have devoted my life to helping people reduce the side effects to their skills so that they can become happier, more vibrant people.

But it's the ups and downs of my own life, in particular the years I spent fighting for my reputation and future as a doctor, ultimately successfully, that have put these tools to the test. I can tell you, from my vantage point on the other side of the shift, that there is no life circumstance that can't be turned to good.

Shift your perspective, and you might just find yourself in a whole new paradigm.

About Dr. Sprouse

Dr. Sprouse was born in 1956. He grew up in the mid-Atlantic region in a row house with his parents and four siblings. He started working as a newspaper boy at the age of eleven but decided by age thirteen that he wanted to be a doctor to help people.

In high school he earned accolades as the captain of the wrestling team, scholastic athlete of the year, and salutatorian of his class. He attended George Washington University for his bachelor's degree. He continued his studies at GWU for his medical school training, where he graduated in the top 10 percent of his class.

Dr. Sprouse set up his medical practice in an underserved area in the Eastern Shore of Maryland. During his years in practice, he has worked hard to be a relatable physician to his thousands of patients. He has had a lot of stress throughout the years and has employed his own stress reducers.

He sings karaoke, plays pickup basketball, travels, reads, and loves to dress up for Halloween. He has two adult children from his previous marriage, and his current wife, Terri, has two children from her previous marriage. He has two grandchildren, so far.

This is his second book; his first book is titled *Highway to Your Happy Place: A Roadmap to Less Stress*, and there are plans for many more books in the future. He is leading seminars on stress reduction. There is an online course for those who can't attend in person. He feels his unique and varied background and his skill for translating complex medical issues for his patients are the right combination to help people live a better life and spend more time in their happy place.

CHAPTER 14

BLOOMING INTO YOUR BEST SELF

I'm Living Proof That It's Never Too Late

By Jean Janki Samaroo

I am not the person I was when I was younger.

Back then, I was negative. I was selfish. I used to want to get things, to have things. I was focused on money and popularity and the trappings that go with them.

I was into worldly success—but not anymore.

Now I am focused on giving things. They're not often big things, at least not to me. A smile to a stranger, a flower arrangement to a friend, a music accompaniment at a hospital program for patients, music for a birthday party.

They make people happy, these things. That's my goal at this point in my life. It was a journey to get here, of course. All of life is a journey. There are no destinations, only pathways to who you are always becoming. In coming to know myself, I've reframed my idea of success. I'm no longer looking to be successful the way the world defines it. I define it to be what I feel about myself.

I will turn seventy-five this year, so I'm a bit of a late bloomer. I'm also living proof that it's never too late to change your mindset and become who you want to be.

Here are the tenets I live by:

1. Define success your own way.

I know now that if I want to be successful, I must serve others. I don't mean in a transactional way, but in a way that returns nothing to me but happiness and fulfillment. Giving provides more joy than getting ever could.

For example, this past holiday season, I decided that none of my friends need me to go to the store and buy them something as a sign of my friendship. Instead, I made them each a beautiful flower arrangement. It made them happy. In turn, it gave me great joy.

I try to ease the load for someone else whenever I can. A couple of years ago, after a concert at the University of Toronto, near where I live, I was hungry, but I didn't have much time before I had to be somewhere else. I did something I don't often do—I went to McDonald's and bought a burger and fries.

As I was eating, I noticed a man sitting a couple of rows of seats over. He didn't have a thing to eat. He wasn't being disruptive or anything. He was just sitting there. But I could tell he was hungry.

After I finished, I took five dollars to the manager, pointed out the man, and asked if she would buy him a meal and drink, filling in with McDonald's funds where mine didn't cover. She went to the register, and I went to leave, stopping first in the washroom.

When I came out, the man was gone, but a crumpled-up wrapper lay where he had been sitting. When I got outside, I saw him walking, with a drink in his hand.

I stopped and took in the joy I felt. That's the feeling I want to have always.

2. Embrace the journey.

I am both an author and an artist, but it took me decades to believe it, let alone say it.

As a young girl, I told myself I would grow up to be an author. I took my first job as a teenager in a library in Guyana. I went on to study library arts at Ryerson University in Toronto and worked in several university and public libraries before I had my son.

My younger self believed I would write lots and lots of books in my life. As it does sometimes, life got in the way of that goal, and I didn't publish a single book until 2020.

That year, I published two: *Late Blooms: Inspiration for Seniors* and *Making New Friends*, a children's book.

By then, I had been blogging for many years, but I never thought of myself as an author. *Late Blooms: A Blog Inspired by Late Bloomers* is about life and art and friends and women's rights and things that catch my attention. But that didn't make me an author, did it?

Throughout my life I've dabbled in art. A couple of years ago, I got more serious about it, both taking photographs and painting. In 2020 I used my own art and photos to illustrate *Late Blooms: Inspiration for Seniors*.

One day, on a whim, I sent one of my pieces to the ARTBOX. PROJECTS, an international exhibition launched in 2015 in Switzerland "to promote artists from all over the world and to offer them an easily accessible platform on which they can present themselves and their art to the public."

I'm proud to say that my work has been displayed with the show in Zurich, Miami, and New York. It's been one of the highlights of my life and a reason I call myself an artist.

In 2023, more than twenty-three years after my father's death, I published a book of his poems called *A Gift of Love: Poems*. His eldest grandson wrote the foreword, I wrote the introduction, and some of the artwork inside was done by his youngest son. I designed the cover art and edited the book. It is the very definition of a labor of love.

Today, I'm planning a couple more book projects. One will be written for the children of Guyana and will feature the local flowers and birds that will look familiar to them. It's important for them to see themselves and where they live reflected in the books they read. It's also important for them to see the beauty of where they live.

I'm also starting a project for the indigenous people of Guyana who, like most indigenous people, were looked down upon as I was growing up. I want to do something to honor them.

These projects are not about the money. They are about giving of myself and giving back. In fact, all my work at this point in my life is to share with others while I'm still here and able to. I am enjoying the experiences of doing these projects and getting to know people along the way.

3. Practice gratitude.

I didn't understand when I was younger how much I have to be grateful for. Like so many young people, I was just certain that everything I had in my life was because of what I had done to make it happen.

That is, of course, nonsense.

I have come to understand that everything I am and everything I have is because of those who came before me and made sacrifices so that I would have a good life. This has translated into a gratitude practice that honors my ancestors, my family, and my friends every day in every way.

I'm grateful for the sacrifices of my great-grandparents who came from India to Guyana in search of a better life. It must have been terrifying to leave everything you know behind, get on a ship to cross a vast ocean in search of more opportunity. Can you imagine?

They arrived in a new land and had to make their way by using their own knowledge and intelligence and, I am certain, by relying on the others who had taken the same journey before and with them.

I am grateful for the sacrifices of my grandparents who built upon what my great-grandparents had done before them. I remember my grandfather, a good and patient man, with great love. My cousin has always said I was my grandfather's favorite. He was absolutely mine.

I learned recently that my grandfather was more than just a kind and gentle man. He was also a gentleman who was very important to Guyana.

As Indians continued to immigrate to Guyana, my grandfather served as something of an immigration officer to them. He wasn't just their interpreter; he was also their counselor, their guide, and the one who helped them learn the ways of Guyana. His guidance and expertise helped smooth the transition for them and enabled them to settle in a new land far from home.

He is remembered today in Guyana because of his work, and I feel grateful to have been loved by such an important man.

I am grateful to my own parents, who sacrificed so much for my brothers and me. They did their best to raise us well and give us what we needed to live full lives.

For example, my lifelong love of music was encouraged by my parents, who bought me a piano when I was young. It must have been so expensive, but it was a sacrifice they were willing to make because they knew how much it meant to me.

That sacrifice has continued to enrich my life. A few years ago I taught myself to play the accordion because I love listening to the sound of the instrument. I wouldn't have been able to do that if I didn't know how to play the piano, a talent my parents recognized and nurtured when I was young.

I find that making connections of gratitude is critical to helping me feel a part of the world and a descendant of my past. It also reminds me that independence—which I believed for much of my life was the goal we were all striving for—is a facade. We are all interdependent. We rely on each other for sustenance of our souls.

Take, for example, my youngest brother, Mitra, who has been instrumental to me in this part of my life journey.

He is the original blogger in our family and was my inspiration. When I finally decided I had something to say and told him I wanted to start writing a blog, he set me up. In essence, he started it for me.

In doing so, he gave me an outlet for my passions and a way to express myself through writing, photography, and art. It's not only an opportunity for me to explore my own interests and ideas, but also a way for me to share myself with others.

It's been enormously life-giving to me.

My first blog post came after I went to a butterfly conservatory and took beautiful pictures. I wrote two short passages to go with the pictures but realized they were too short to stand as blog posts on their own. Mitra encouraged me to combine them and post the resulting piece with the pictures, which I did.

I've done hundreds of blog posts since then, providing a running commentary on life for many years. This outlet has led me to explore other ways to express my passions and enrich my own life, along with the lives of others.

Mitra has abilities that I don't have, particularly in the technology sphere. A few years ago, he put together a website for me, which the blog is now a part of, where I can express myself in all the ways I want to. There you can find all my passions in one place. It feels like home.

We have always been close, Mitra and I. Sharing a love of writing and music and being each other's number one fan as we pursue our individual endeavors has brought us even closer. It is so important in this world to have someone like he and I have in each other. Our relationship has enriched us as siblings but also as humans.

4. Peace and happiness come from within.

These days I believe that nothing external will make me happy or give me peace. It all comes from a life force within. I am focused on feeding and caring for my inner being.

It's been a long journey to get to this place, but I am here, at a fulfilling stop on the journey I will continue for as long as I live.

I focus on art. I meditate. I exercise and move my body.

I've learned to set and keep boundaries. I no longer try to please people, especially at the expense of myself.

I used to think that I had unlimited energy. Now I realize I have only so much energy, and I've cut back on things that don't give me peace.

I believe in a higher power, of course, but I'm not looking for a savior. I know that staying focused on the things that bring me joy and give me peace is what will save me.

As is true for all of us, the challenges and hardships I have had in my life could have done one of two things: broken me or made me stronger. I'm proud to say I am much stronger because of them and that I am able to draw on the strength they've brought me. I know that when faced with the choice to stay down or pick myself up, I consistently find the strength to get up and move on.

I also have developed the ability to reframe an experience or idea. Nothing is set in stone when it comes to how you think about it. You are in control of how you see and respond to it. When you know how to reframe it, it changes your life in profound ways.

My favorite bit of reframing has to do with how I define death. Death is not when we stop breathing. Death is when we stop caring and sharing, when we fight with each other, when we discount humanity.

That's when we stop living.

About Jean

Jean Janki Samaroo is a vibrant soul nestled in the heart of Toronto, Canada, alongside her beloved husband and their cherished Ragdoll cat. At seventy-four years young, Jean embodies the essence of a lifelong learner, embracing every moment as an opportunity for growth and exploration.

Her journey through academia led her to Ryerson University, where she delved into the realm of library arts and later became a certified TESL/TEFL instructor. However, her thirst for knowledge extends far beyond the confines of traditional education, as she continuously immerses herself in the diverse tapestry of life's teachings.

Jean wears many hats with grace and passion. An avid blogger, author, editor, photographer, and artist, she paints her experiences with words that resonate across diverse topics, mirroring the breadth of her eclectic interests.

In the cozy corners of her home, Jean's heart finds solace in the company of Ali Baba, her faithful feline companion, who has been a constant source of joy since his tender days at nine weeks old. While Ali Baba reigns as her first love, Jean's wanderlust knows no bounds, having traversed every continent save Africa—a dream she holds dear and hopes to fulfill in the near future.

Jean's literary endeavors have garnered acclaim, with two printed works, *Late Blooms: Inspiration for Seniors* and the enchanting children's picture book *Making New Friends*, earning Firebird Book Awards and gracing the shelves of Amazon. Additionally, her editorial prowess shines through in the compilation and editing of *Strong Women Make History*, an e-book commemorating the historic Biden/Harris inauguration and International Women's Day in 2021.

Driven by a fervent belief in the power of women's voices, Jean advocates for their recognition and reverence across all spheres of society. Through her poignant contributions to various platforms, such as Medium, Simply Woman magazine, and Brown Girl Diary, she amplifies narratives that celebrate and empower women worldwide.

Beyond the written word, Jean's altruistic spirit finds expression in her myriad volunteer roles, from nurturing young minds in Toronto's public school classrooms to offering English lessons to refugees from diverse corners of the globe. Her accordion melodies have brought smiles to faces in hospital wards, senior centers, and community gatherings, illustrating the transformative impact of selfless acts of kindness.

Read Jean's blog posts at https://lateblooms.jeanjankisamaroo.com/1/web.

CHAPTER 15

THE ALOHA SPIRIT IN CONSTRUCTION

How Honesty and Kindness Helped a Company Grow

By Lance Luke

"The building repair was too expensive," they said. "Besides," they added, "it doesn't look that bad."

I hear that a lot in my line of work as a construction engineer in Hawaii. On the Hawaiian Islands of paradise, people think buildings last forever. They ignore signs of danger. After all, there are waves to conquer, beaches to explore, mountains to climb, and waterfalls to chase. Who has the time—or the money—to tackle every problem? We're too busy having fun in the Hawaiian sun!

Honestly, though, we are all like that sometimes. We hear a "knocking sound" in the car's engine and assume it will disappear. We feel a pain in a tooth and pray it's just temporary.

We see a weed in the yard and think it's likely the only one.

We tend to ignore problems. We place them in the back of our minds. We stubbornly fight to forget about them. As for preventive maintenance, who has time for that!

Of course, problems usually persist and often worsen. Similar to a small snowball cascading down the side of a cliff, they can grow into a more formidable force and soon, into an avalanche of chaos. The thump in the car's engine may escalate into a critical mechanical failure. The tooth pain may be a warning sign of a significant cavity. The weed in the yard could be the first of hundreds.

And the crack in the wall could escalate into a structural compromise, endangering the stability of the entire building. It also could turn a nominal expense into a financial headache. That happened the day I visited the owners of a twenty-story condominium five blocks from Honolulu's beaches. The condo had an issue. I was contacted as the building expert.

It was like any other day in the Aloha State. A radiant yellow sun in a sky painted with hues of coral and azure had cast a golden glow over the turquoise waters of the Pacific. A gentle trade wind whispered through the swaying palm trees outside the condo, carrying the sweet scent of plumeria blossoms. The rhythmic sound of ocean waves served as a backdrop to the day's unfolding events. Honolulu's streets bustled with locals and visitors, each immersed in the island's laid-back atmosphere. It was a palate for the senses. Unfortunately, my diagnosis that day was not as pleasant as the island's natural charm.

After we exchanged smiles and handshakes, the owners led me to the corner of the high-rise condominium building. They were concerned. "What do you think?" one of them asked.

The condo, built five decades ago, had seen several small cracks growing larger through a concrete wall. I could easily fix it right then, but from their viewpoint it was worth delaying.

"How much will it cost to repair?"

"Perhaps…$20,000," I replied. Their eyes grew big, as if I had told them a shocking secret.

"That's too expensive," one of them replied.

"It doesn't look too bad," said the other. "We'll wait." I smiled and shrugged, acknowledging the financial weight of the situation while not hiding the seriousness of the structural problem.

Two years later they called back. "We're ready to move forward with the repair."

But the problem had worsened. Like an untreated cavity, the once manageable cracks in the condo's concrete wall had expanded into something that would now cost far more to fix, estimated at

$200,000. In barely twenty-four months, the cost of the repair had grown tenfold. No doubt, it would be expensive.

I took no joy in sharing the shocking news. But I had been honest—a trait that has served me well in my work. It's been a key to my success. I want to shoot straight with people. I want my word to be my bond. If the structure has minimal problems—or no issues—I acknowledge it. Yet if major repairs are necessary, I dare not remain silent.

This commitment to honesty is a professional strategy and a reflection of my core values. I strive for transparency and integrity in an industry where advice can sometimes be ambiguous, if not plain dishonest. If done with compassion, being forthright by delivering tough news is the only real response. It even may include acknowledging when things haven't gone as planned. After all, demonstrating humility is not a sign of weakness but a sign of authenticity.

The construction management profession requires honesty— *needs* honesty. Trust between the condo managers and me is necessary for problems to be solved and buildings to be properly repaired. If significant issues are not inspected and repaired as they occur, then major safety problems can quickly arise. A condo with an unrepaired crack can fall apart and endanger its occupants.

The potential danger isn't theoretical.

In 2021 ninety-eight people died when a twelve-story condominium in Surfside, Florida, collapsed. Investigators blamed the tragedy on a "severe structural deficiency" in its pool deck that did not meet building codes. The building was forty years old.

In 2023 three people died in Davenport, Iowa, when a six-story apartment complex partially collapsed. There, investigators blamed the incident on improper support for a wall that was under construction.

In 2017 four people died and thirteen were injured, including an emergency worker, when a thirty-six-story condo in Honolulu caught fire. The units did not have a sprinkler system.

Thankfully, I was not involved in any of those tragedies. But my life's goal is to ensure similar catastrophes don't occur on my watch.

A condo owner with decades-old cast iron pipes called once, asking my advice on stopping the frequent leaks.

"Replace all the pipes in your building," I told him.

"We don't have the money for that," he responded.

Several months later a main pipe burst in his building, impacting twenty units and leading to $500,000 in repairs. I call it "stepping over a dollar to pick up a penny." Too often condo owners kick the proverbial can down the road, believing the repairs can wait. When problems escalate, insurance companies cancel policy coverage and rates go up.

My family instilled in me the value of honesty from an early age. They also handed down a passion for construction.

My grandfather and uncle were involved in real estate, a popular career path in Chinese culture. I am Chinese Hawaiian, and in that society you don't purchase real estate to sell it—you purchase real estate to make money to buy more. Renting is king in our Chinese culture.

My grandfather owned multiple rental properties, placing me and my brother in charge of maintaining them. It was educational on-the-job training that taught us many skills, including carpentry, roofing, plumbing, and electrical wiring—all while we were in our teens. I repaired houses as my friends played on the beach and surfed the waves. I was a skinny twelve-year-old who painted walls, nailed shingles, fixed floors, and stopped leaks. Sure, I found time to go surfing too, but I also learned valuable skills that laid the groundwork for my future.

Back then, there was no Google or YouTube. You learned construction by trial and error. My brother and I often took a pipe or electrical wire to the hardware store, asking the workers for advice on how to complete that day's task. We needed their knowledge and how-to. Thankfully, they were more than willing to assist.

After earning my civil engineering degree in college and my real estate license, my uncle—the state's largest real estate developer—hired me as his construction manager. We built highrise buildings and condominiums. We constructed subdivisions. During my ten years working under him I learned everything I could. It was a natural transition to launching my own company, Construction Management Inspection LLC.

Advice from my father has been my foundation. "What's the secret to success?" I asked him once, expecting a lecture about education or hard work.

His answer surprised me: "Helping people." If you do that, he said, then money will follow. In Hawaii we call it the "aloha spirit." We lead with love. My goal in life isn't to make money. It's to help people.

Like a well-crafted tool, I've built my business on three basic precepts: (1) helping others, (2) being kind, and (3) displaying honesty. With over four decades under my belt as a construction manager and successful business owner, it's safe to say my father's philosophy has proved true.

One time the governing board of a condo association called and asked if I could look at their building and advise them on potential maintenance and upgrades.

"Of course," I responded.

I walked around the property with the building manager and several board members, pointing out a few problems and suggesting possible fixes. I took pictures and wrote notes. A few days later I sent the board an official report, expecting a call back to schedule the largely minor repairs.

They didn't call back. Until, that is, five years later. "We're ready to get the work done," one of the board members said. It had been so long that I nearly responded, "Who are you?" But then I remembered.

"What made you call me back?" I asked.

"You're the only building inspector who gave us an honest

opinion," the woman said. "Everyone else gave us a sales pitch and quoted their hourly rate. Others tried to pressure us."

My honesty had led to a $120,000 contract—half a decade after they first called.

My only "sales pitch" was kindness and honesty. This approach has helped me find a niche in the Hawaii market of inspecting and managing construction for properties, condominiums, and buildings. It's an approach I use with the competition as well. I'm friends with my competitors. We meet for lunch and share ideas. We don't argue or fight. Instead, we laugh and collaborate, recognizing that mutual respect and camaraderie contribute to a better construction industry.

"I don't have anything to hide," I often tell them.

Sometimes they give me a puzzled look, wondering why I sound so different from other managers. I tell them this: "We don't need money-hungry, fly-by-night operators. We need honest, competent people in every industry, especially among construction managers." I tell the younger ones, "One day I'll retire, and maybe you'll take over."

My clients have my cell phone number, and I answer their calls as a first priority. I don't want them waiting on answers.

When a project begins, I'm on site, at dawn, when the construction workers arrive. I don't hand the leadership to someone else, but I don't micromanage, either. Clients sometimes have differing views with the contractors—and vice versa—and it is my job to bring about a solid understanding of the project's scope and to forge an agreement. Although I represent the client owner or condominium board, it is my job to clearly communicate the work progress, complete the project on time in cooperation with contractors, and get them paid on time as promised.

I go to bat for my clients. Once, after helping a town-house complex client install new top-of-the-line roofing, I noticed a strange white powder atop the shingles. I did not know what it was. The manufacturer's representative didn't, either.

"It'll wash off in the rain," he assured me. "Give it six months."

But six months later the white stain had not vanished.

"Give it another year," the roofing rep told me.

I was skeptical but nevertheless agreed to wait another twelve months. A year later that white stain had not disappeared. Once again, I contacted the roof representative.

"We're filing a warranty claim against the manufacturer, alleging the shingles are defective," I told him.

I wanted to see a wrong made right. Months later, and after dozens of emails, I was preparing to send a shingle sample to a laboratory for testing when—suddenly—the roofing manufacturer changed its mind and relented. Long story short, the town houses were given new roofs, saving the owners $275,000.

The key to success is simple. It's the same precepts we were taught growing up. Help others. Be kind. Stay honest. If you do that, success will follow.

About Lance

Celebrity Expert, Hawaii Building Expert

Lance Luke has been in the construction industry for over forty-three years. He is a former general contractor and worked as a construction and project manager for real estate development companies. Currently he owns an independent construction consulting company, Construction Management Inspection LLC. His experience is in design, construction inspections, construction management, reserve studies, and real estate development. He is a sought-after national building expert.

Lance has held the following designations for many years:

- Certified Construction Inspector (CCI)
- Certified Construction Project Manager (CCPM)
- Certified Construction Consultant (CCC)

Lance serves as an expert witness on construction and real estate litigation cases. He was formally an advisory board member for the State of Hawaii Regulated Industries Complaints Office, as an expert consultant (for over fifteen years). His expertise was in helping to resolve complaints filed with the Contractors License Board.

He has written numerous articles on construction and inspection, which are published in both local and national print media. He conducts up to eighty presentations a year to the construction, real estate, and property management industry, including educational webinars and seminars.

Lance is an approved federal HUD construction inspector. He is also listed as one of America's Premier Experts and Marquis Who's Who in America 70th Anniversary Edition. He is also a business mentor, a community-service volunteer, a professional speaker, and a two-time best-selling author.

Lance is a former member of the Structural Engineers Association of Hawaii and the American Bar Association, serving on the Real Property/Probate Law Division and the Forum for the Construction Industry. He is a current member of the National Fire Protection Association.

Lance is also an owner of several other firms that include a digital marketing company, a publishing company, a business directory, an

AI company, a VA services provider, and a university that offers online classes.

His two webinar series have a loyal and growing following: askbuildingexpert.now.site and askmarketingexperts.now.site.

He is an award-winning movie producer and is currently working on producing long- and short-form videos for his various business ventures and his clients.

Lastly, he is a professional musician and plays guitar in a music group called Kolea. The group plays songs ranging from Broadway tunes and jazz standards to bossa nova and classic contemporary music.

CHAPTER 16

EMERGE POSITIVE

*My Journey from Automatic Living
to the Other Side of Fear*

By Deanne Lewis

W hen my best friend got sick, traditional medicine offered few answers. Then she began working with a naturopathic doctor and his wife, a spiritual teacher. My friend, amazed by the results, told me I should see this spiritual teacher as well.

"Why?" I immediately thought. "I'm doing just fine."

I was a very linear thinker then, having grown up in a time when seeking out therapy or any help was perceived as weakness. I never even sought out mentors, because I thought it was my job to shoulder whatever life threw at me. To push through. At the time, it never dawned on me I could go further and learn more (and actually enjoy the ride) if I worked with someone who could guide me along my path.

Early on my parents taught me the importance of a strong personal ethic, and I used that as my barometer and guide in both my professional and personal lives. In my twenties life was pretty good to me. I believed all I had to do was show up and do a good job, and somehow life would work out. And that worked for a while. I had a good marriage, a great job with a good income, and a wonderful circle of friends. But I operated under what I now call "automatic living." Get up. Get ready for your day. Go to work. Come home. Enjoy the evening. Go to bed. Rinse and repeat.

I *reacted* to whatever life threw at me and made the best choices

I could. That was my life for many years. Some years were good. Others weren't. But I continued to keep my head down and plow a path forward, navigating whatever life brought me and believing that was what I was supposed to do.

That life included a marriage to my high school sweetheart. I put him at the center of my world. Everything else was secondary, including me, my career, friendships, and any personal interests. So imagine my shock and devastation one day when he told me he didn't love me "as a husband should love a wife" and left.

After the divorce I was numb, aimless, and wandering. I felt like a failure. I had no idea about who I was or what I wanted in life. Despite my enormous debt, I continued to spend. I needed to be out of the house as much as possible. Distracted as much as possible. I went out to restaurants, bought new clothes, flew around the country visiting friends, and went into further debt trying to find happiness. It wasn't wise, but it's how I survived.

Honestly, when my friend suggested I see that spiritual teacher, I was afraid. This woman didn't fit into my way of thinking. Looking back, I was actually afraid of what she might uncover if I *did* work with her. It felt much safer to just figure this out on my own.

One day while dropping off my friend at her house, the teacher met us at the car. She didn't usually do this, but not wanting to be rude, I chatted with her on a patch of grass outside the home. After a few pleasantries the spiritual teacher took two fingers, pressed them gently against my chest, and said, "Your heart is closed."

The second her fingers touched me, I immediately collapsed in tears. She saw me. Not the mask I'd been wearing, but *me*. Years of pent-up sadness came spilling out, and although I was afraid, I knew this person was someone I needed to speak with.

We ended up working together for seven years across two different states. First, I came to her as a student to work through my own healing. Then she taught me to move forward as a teacher and healer myself.

Through my time with her I learned pain is not something

to fear or to avoid. It's a teacher. It wakes people up from automatic living. By working with her, I was able to release the pain of my divorce and to find my life purpose and personal connection to God.

How I Emerged Positive from the Greatest Trauma of My Life

After seven years of intensive work on myself, I came to many realizations. These are the lessons that helped pull me from the fog and darkness of my divorce into the light of intentional living:

Everything starts with mindset.

I tell people now my divorce was the worst *and* best thing that ever happened to me. It knocked me facedown, but that massive fall woke me up. It picked me up and put me on a different path, changing every area of my life.

As I became more intentional about how I lived and thought, even my relationship to money changed. I started to see the abundant world we live in and that there is truly enough for everyone. I learned money is like a river that runs through you. It's a tool for you to use. Your belief system can open or close the flow. It's truly up to us.

Your mindset and belief system are the foundation for *all* aspects of your life. Through this journey I learned automatic living and a scarcity mindset were not the only options. I learned I hold the power, as do you, to create an amazing life.

And I learned it all starts with mindset.

Pain made me more self-aware.

After working with my teacher, I quickly learned I had been operating my life under a "social mask," and it was getting heavier by the week. I held these beliefs about who I was supposed to be, how I was supposed to think, and what I was supposed to want. I certainly didn't remember creating these. They were simply there—and running my life.

I was shocked to realize I was essentially sleepwalking. I thought reacting to whatever crossed my path was just how life was and I really didn't have a say.

Today, I think of this as being in an inner tube, floating down the river of life, and reacting to whatever comes. Swift rapids. Gentle waves. Large falls. We just hold on, hoping for the best. But we never realize something important: the river is just three feet deep. We can stand up and walk out whenever we want.

Pain made that realization possible for me. Don't run from it. Embrace what it's teaching you.

Start with a centering morning routine.

With a shift in mindset you can create a life you love, and one foundational starting point for me was my spiritual morning routine. It's different for everyone, and there's no wrong way to do it, but it's simply a series of actions that help you have the right mindset for the day. It's a way to focus and to re-center yourself every morning.

Even if it's only ten minutes, do something that allows you to clear your mind and to connect to your internal source. Meditating. Listening to uplifting music. Journaling. Visualizing. Reading something positive.

For me, affirmations have the most impact because they reset my mind. If I wake up in a negative headspace, they shift me out of it. They're also short and easy to read daily, so they're easy to make a habit of. This is why I created Emerge Positive.

This positive mindset affects your choices, and it impacts what you attract to yourself. This quite literally changes what each day brings you.

The net appears after you jump.

A few years after my divorce I summoned the courage to answer a deep pull within me to relocate across the country to Atlanta. I tried to make this bold life move in a logical way. I'm a planner by nature, so I wanted to find a new job that would pay to relocate me. I already had a great job as a Warner Bros. executive, and I didn't want to just throw that away without a good replacement.

But opportunity after opportunity passed me by. After eighteen months of a job search I started to lose faith. Maybe this wasn't what I was supposed to be doing. So I went to church and prayed. It was January 2008, and I swear I heard God himself tell me it was time to go. Now.

Shaking to my core, I told my boss the very next day, I was moving to Atlanta. I didn't know anyone there. I had no job and a ton of debt. I just hoped my boss would let me stay on until they found my replacement.

As soon as I told him, everything miraculously fell into place. Instead of just staying on until they found my replacement, they promoted me, giving me a raise and a new three-year contract. The apartment I wanted suddenly became available. After almost two years, my move was now happening in six weeks. It all lined up perfectly because I took a leap of faith.

Beliefs + Perception = Choice of Action

Our beliefs, both positive and negative, are taught to us in childhood. They are our thoughts. These come from our parents, extended family, teachers, coaches, neighbors, and anyone with influence in our lives. Some examples include:

- In order to be loved, I have to play small.
- I'm not lovable.
- Women can't handle money.
- Money is a bad thing. I'm not supposed to want it.
- I'm not good enough.
- I have bad genetics; I'll never be thin.
- If I get angry, I'm a bad person.
- I'm not beautiful, so I'm not worthy.

The problem? Most of us don't stop to question our beliefs. We just act on them or, rather, react to them. This set of beliefs you didn't consciously choose (and that is likely invisible to you) determines your perception of life.

Think of your perception as your personal filter. It takes situations, people, and circumstances that come across your path, and creates a reasoning and a story about why anything is happening to you. And in the end it creates the words you choose to speak.

Those two things together (beliefs and perception, which I call mindset) drive the action you choose to take. And let's just cut to the chase: The actions you choose are the life you live. When you piece together each action you take, that's you creating your day, week, year, and, yes, even your life. Taking action is paramount if you want to improve your life, and mindset is what creates action.

Understanding the negative core beliefs within you requires investigation. This is where a coach can help. As a starting point, though, the easiest way for you to begin is to look at your life because *life always proves our beliefs true.*

In my case, my biggest fear was being alone. I didn't understand it at the time, but I believed I was unlovable. The idea of my husband leaving was terrifying, and I believed I couldn't financially support myself without him. Life brought this front and center. Our beliefs always show up.

If you don't think you're lovable, you're likely single or in an unfulfilling relationship. (I've been there!) If you don't believe you deserve money or believe you shouldn't want money because it's bad, you likely don't have any savings or you have a poor relationship with money. (This was also me!)

Take the time to look at your life's results. They all began with a core belief.

One of my favorite teachers is Louise Hay. She has a famous saying: "A belief is just a thought, and a thought can be changed." Once you can see the belief, you can make the choice to change it. This is how you take responsibility for your life. In my experience once I took that responsibility, every single aspect of my life changed for the better. I started each day in anticipation of what amazing new thing would happen next. It was like being in a game of miracles!

This was not some special gift afforded just to me. This is for everyone who wants it. When you're able to open up your heart and become more connected with God, you can see, enjoy, and experience this incredible place we get to live in and life overall in a very different way.

That doesn't mean it's all rainbows. There's still pain and difficulty, but instead of asking why something is happening *to* you, you can reframe the question. What am I supposed to be learning from this? Seeing a purpose behind the pain helps you emerge through it faster, stronger, and better.

Emerging Positive Is Accessible to Everyone

I stayed in Atlanta for four years. During that time, I diligently worked on my personal growth. It was like a master class. I developed a strong spiritual life. I met and helped people all over the world. I paid off over $30,000 in debt. I got in the best shape of my life. (Thank you, Pilates!) I also met the love of my life, who is now my husband.

Today, I live in San Diego, a place I'd dreamed of living in for over twenty years. I live with my husband and stepson, whom I absolutely adore, in a beautiful home. I have no money worries, as I used my newfound money principles to create a nice nest egg. I am genuinely happy and at peace with life. (Although menopause has thrown me a twenty-pound curveball, and a glass of wine—or two—is still my favorite way to unwind. What can I say? I'm still a work in progress.)

I created a new life with new rules and a new perception that drove new actions and positive outcomes. I can honestly say I love my life.

If you want that too, take the time to investigate who you are now. Then, ask yourself what you want. Who do you want to become? Are you on the path to get there? What do you need to change? What are your passions? Your gifts? How can you be of service? What does success look like to you? It's never too late to grab hold of the reins of your life and create a life you love.

My goal is to reach as many people as possible, helping them to create positive change in their lives through a shift in mindset. The more of us who do that, the better our world becomes. When one changes, we are all impacted.

Life is one giant miracle. There is so much abundance, love, opportunity, and personal growth awaiting you, and life is so much more fun when you actually participate in it.

So what are you waiting for?

You can *emerge positive*!

About Deanne

Deanne is the founder and CEO of Emerge Positive, a mindset company helping individuals shift their mindset and improve their lives. Working with both corporations and individuals alike, Deanne is introducing the importance and impact of mindset. Her talks and teachings uplift, inspire, and demonstrate ways to bring self-love, prosperity, freedom, relationship, and positive perspective into your life.

With extensive corporate and leadership experience within Fortune 500 companies, Deanne offers a unique perspective to companies and individuals looking to elevate their career and lives.

She created Connect by Emerge Positive, a corporate subscription to a daily digital feed of positive mindset quotes delivered directly to your desktop. The daily feed inspires positive thoughts to promote productivity, positive work culture, mindset, happiness, and overall well-being.

Deanne also offers uplifting keynote talks and coaching that deliver positive mental health and improved results in the workplace and at home.

For individuals, EP Insider by Emerge Positive and EP online classes will help people implement positive change across all areas of life. Deanne is the author of the book *Emerge Positive* and writes Emerge Positive daily on social media as well as a weekly Sunday newsletter. Go to **www.emergepositive.com/GetStarted** to sign up and learn more.

Deanne lives in San Diego with her Navy veteran husband and teenage stepson. She spends her free time reading, exercising, cooking, and learning about wine, travel, and real estate.

To work with Deanne and learn how Emerge Positive can help you, go to **www.emergepositive.com/GetStarted**.

CHAPTER 17

TRIUMPH IN TURMOIL

A Journey of Loss, Resilience, and Renewal

By Willie Diefenbach-Jones

A TERRIBLE DAY STARTS WITH A PHONE CALL

When the independent-living facility call came at seven o'clock that morning, I knew something was terribly wrong. Answering the phone, I learned the news that every child dreads: During the early-morning hours my mother had passed away. At that moment, time stood still. The woman who had been my rock, my confidante, was gone. I had always teased that she would live forever, her spirit a beacon of strength. Yet the harsh reality of mortality had come crashing down with brutal force.

My mother was more than a parent; she was my mentor, my source of inspiration. Her unwavering determination and infectious laughter had shaped my very being. She loved to read and instilled the love of reading not only in me but also in many others. She knew how to make good things happen and did exactly that. Raised amid the trials and immense challenges of the Great Depression, she met a diverse array of obstacles and scarcities head-on, fostering within herself an unyielding determination that knew no bounds. This resilient mindset became a cornerstone of her teachings, which she imparted to many others and me with unwavering conviction.

However, that was part of her story and part of what made her a strong lady. Things had gotten difficult over the last few years, especially as her health and faculties started their gradual decline.

I wanted her to move closer to me in Texas. However, she wanted nothing to do with that, as her friends, church and clubs were all in Illinois and she didn't want to leave that behind. After all, she was a fiercely independent retired schoolteacher and a farmer's wife. Most recently, she had started to lose her hearing, requiring a hearing aid, which she thought of as a nuisance and wore inconsistently. This became a challenge for everyone who interacted with her. I just kept coming back to the awful feeling of how sudden her passing felt, and I didn't have one last opportunity to say, "Thank you for being a great mom," and, most importantly, "I love you."

Being a naturally organized person, once I recovered from the immediate shock, I started making lists. Creating order is how my brain works. Death comes with a lot of emotion, but I could also see that there was a lot that I needed to do.

I knew that it was up to me to step up and take charge of everything that needed to be done. Someone had to arrange the funeral. Family and friends needed to be notified. Any last affairs needed to be taken care of. All of it amounted to a tall order for anyone, even a naturally organized person, to handle.

But the more I tried to push through, a harsh reality struck me: The pain of my loss was awfully hard to ignore. I got through some of my to-do list, checking off the most important things, but before long I was exhausted. I had to let go.

It was a Friday. I had to get through this grief and pick up and keep going.

THAT ONLY GETS WORSE

That evening my husband was due to go on a hog hunting trip with a few of his buddies. In light of our family's recent loss, we talked briefly about whether he should go. There was a lot to do; everyone was in shock. I knew that I was in bad shape, still reeling from the previous day's call, but I assured him everything was going to be OK.

"Go on," I said. "You paid for the trip, and you have been looking forward to it." I felt good knowing he was going to do something he enjoyed. With my word, my husband went.

If I knew then what I know now, however, I would have never let him walk out that door.

The next day was a Saturday. Our son was playing high school baseball. He was scheduled to play in a doubleheader at a nearby field and had gotten a ride to the field with a friend.

With some welcome time alone, I set about taking care of some tasks. Keeping busy was always a way to keep me going. I decided to prepare some food in the slow cooker to eat when we arrived home from the games. We would have something hot, delicious, and healthy and not have to scramble to figure out dinner. Then, suddenly, there was a knock on the door. I thought it was one of our neighbors, but when I paused to look out the window, I saw something entirely unexpected.

A state police car. Parked outside my house.

Thinking that maybe the police were here to talk about one of my neighbors, I answered the front door, where I found an officer.

"Can I come in?" he asked.

His tone was solemn. Immediately suspicious, I took a step back. My big dog, picking up on my increasing tension, started growling.

"Why did he want to come inside? What is going on?"

That was when he told me. My husband had been killed. With those words, a terrible wave of shock washed over me. If the feeling of shock over my mother's loss the day before had snuck up on me, then this one was a tsunami, nearly knocking me off my feet.

I managed to get out the question, What had happened? The officer, who could see I was clearly distressed, explained that my husband was killed in a helicopter crash. He and the pilot had died instantly.

The shock I experienced was overwhelming. My immediate thoughts were, "Why my husband?" He was very intelligent and had made many contributions in the world of engineering. He was a great husband and father. He was a really good person. When I told the police officer that my mother died yesterday, he assumed I meant the year prior, that yesterday was the anniversary. After explaining that no, my mother had in fact died the day before, he got really serious, suggesting that I call someone.

It wasn't a good idea for me to be alone.

He was right.

GREAT FRIENDS

The morning after the day my husband died, I could hardly get myself out of bed. After experiencing two of the worst possible days a person can, my mind drifted to the inevitable question: What could possibly happen next?

Whatever it was, I didn't know, but I couldn't bear to see it. So, I drew the covers over my head, rolled over, and tried to make it all go away.

But the dog needed a walk, so I had to get up and open the back door. What I saw outside took my breath away: A group of my friends and neighbors had gathered. After learning of my tragedies, they were there to support me in whatever way I needed.

I may not have wanted to get out of bed. Now I had a reason to get moving.

The friends my husband had been hunting with showed up at the house later. There were a lot of tears and hugs, everyone doing their best to make sense of the awful events.

I also remember the phone ringing off the hook. Everyone from distant friends to family wanted to check in and see how I was. Most of the time, I was humbled to discover they wanted to know whether they could do anything to help.

Help? I was too stunned, at least right away, to really know what I needed. Help came in the most obvious form of food. People would show up at our door offering platters and casseroles, meals we could warm up in a pinch when we found that we were too tired, or too grief-stricken, to know how to care for ourselves.

I had to learn to accept all that outpouring of support, and it's not as easy as it might sound. In fact, it can be overwhelming. One of my friends is a caterer. She brought a huge casserole of chicken and rice to our house. I remember thinking that it was so much food that I hardly knew what we would do with it. I thought it would go to waste, but anyone with a teenage son in sports knows they'll eat as much as you put in front of them. A couple of days later members of my son's baseball team came over after practice. Fortunately I had that chicken and rice that they polished off.

Those hungry, growing boys proved me wrong. I had to learn to see the things before me a little differently now. There was so much of life left to live.

Find Your Focus

Eventually all the food and phone calls stopped. It's not that the people in your life forget about you; however, there comes a point when you have to find your way through.

In those first few months after my tragedies, I chose to ignore the pain. There was an overwhelming amount of it, that's for sure, but delaying the crucial process of actually dealing with it was my path. I don't know that I chose it, but it was the one I found myself on.

I focused on my son, who had his own grief and pain to sort through. He was active in high school baseball. Sports gave him something to hone in on and me something to do. My friends were always there to support me. We would have an occasional girls night out, which was always fun. Mostly, I spent those early grieving months getting things done. I remember that when my father died, my mother cleaned the house from top to bottom in those first couple of weeks. She wanted that house organized and spotless. I didn't go to that extreme, but I certainly felt the need to keep myself active and busy, trying to stay the course.

Nose down. A lot of to-do lists. I wasn't the kind of person who was going to wallow in grief and say, "Woe is me"!

The real grieving process didn't begin until I talked to a widowed friend whose husband had committed suicide. He had taken his life some years back, but the pain she experienced persisted. She was a very cool, analytical person, someone I respect deeply. Something she said struck me out of the blue, and months after those awful days the grieving process kick-started.

Suddenly a group of awful questions flooded me.

What am I going to do?

Can I survive alone? Do I have the skills necessary?

When things broke that my husband usually took care of, what was I going to do? Did I even know whom to call in those situations?

The answers to those questions were yes, of course. I had already started to chart my course. Surviving wasn't ever in doubt. I had the skills and strength to thrive.

But grief has a persistence you don't understand until you experience and tackle it.

ONE THING AT A TIME

My string of tragedies did not end, though. Within six months of my husband's passing I was blindsided by more bad news: I was being laid off from a great job from a company that I loved.

When I first got word, I was absolutely devastated. I had given a lot to that company, and learning that my time there was done hit me hard, knocking me down yet again.

After receiving a good severance package, I decided it was time to consider a crucial life change. I have spent most of my career working in corporate America. I made surprisingly good money, met awesome people, and learned a great deal in the process. But I had also given a lot of myself away in the process of advancing my career. Corporate America owned my life, dictating what hours I worked, where and when I traveled. I missed many of my son's baseball games. I knew that I could no longer feel as if my life was somehow out of my control. Regardless of my desire for security, I couldn't let Corporate America own my life anymore.

While I was fully embracing my grief and in the tender process of reinventing myself, a friend invited me to attend a networking meeting for entrepreneurs. At first, I felt like the proverbial fish out of water, but then I thought of my father. He was a very prosperous, successful farmer. What was a farmer but an entrepreneur in the world of agriculture? Maybe I could be an entrepreneur too.

Something important occurred to me then. I knew these people and how they worked. I knew how to talk to them. Most importantly, I realized that there was a whole entrepreneurial world that I didn't even know about. Maybe I could be successful in that world too.

Attending that meeting did not lead directly to my next job. But from a few of the connections that I made, I took the first step in my next career: consulting. I found that my skills were in demand. That I could bring value to people and companies on my own terms. I also was exposed to the world of MLMs. I never knew such a thing existed, and I couldn't believe the earnings potential, so I jumped on board with an amazing company.

I thought consulting and the MLM world might be a temporary fix. When I looked at the bottom line, however, I was astounded. I made more money my first year out of corporate America than I did at any time in it. There was no going back now. I had made the most difficult change, and I did so by looking inward.

Those tragedies taught me something very important about what happens to me when I get knocked down. I could trust my knowledge of how to get up.

I knew how to put one foot in front of the other and move on.

One step at a time.

About Willie

Meet Willie, the dynamic force who traded in her corporate suit for a life of entrepreneurial excitement! After bidding adieu to over two decades in Corporate America, Willie embarked on a mission to ignite the entrepreneurial spark in others, guiding them toward unlocking multiple income streams. Whether liberating individuals from the 9-to-5 grind or helping others supplement their income for life's special indulgences, Willie's expertise knows no bounds.

Rooted in down-home country values yet armed with corporate acumen, Willie's upbringing on a farm taught her the significance of hard work and meaningful connections. Now she seamlessly integrates these values into her work, infusing them into every endeavor.

As a catalyst for streamlining processes and optimizing efficiency, Willie has driven significant savings for companies while guiding countless individuals to lucrative career opportunities. However, her true passion lies in coaching businesses to flourish by fostering robust relationships. She empowers individuals to leverage personal and professional connections for growth and success.

A lifelong learner, Willie thrives on absorbing knowledge at workshops and seminars, transforming each learning opportunity into actionable strategies. With accolades such as a CPA designation and titles such as Master Six Sigma Black Belt and Master Certified Change Agent, Willie is a formidable force in the business world. Currently pursuing certification as a Transformation Coach, her commitment to personal growth and empowerment knows no bounds.

In her leisure time Willie indulges her passion for food and gardening, experimenting with new recipes and nurturing her garden oasis. When not revolutionizing the business landscape, she enjoys exploring culinary delights with friends and cheering on her beloved Houston Astros during baseball season.

At home Willie takes pride in her role as a devoted mother to her son, Austin, and two cherished dogs, Ghost and Ryder. With her unique blend of warmth and professionalism, Willie is the ultimate ally for taking your business to new heights.

Join Willie on her journey of entrepreneurial triumphs, culinary adventures, and perpetual growth—it's an experience not to be missed!

For those eager to elevate their business and income, connect with Willie at https://linktr.ee/williedj.

CHAPTER 18

BEING SHATTERPROOF

*Your Most Hidden Superpower
and the Missing Peace*

By Patti Boes

They say when the student is ready, the teacher will appear. Sometimes life is that teacher for me, just dropping by to shatter my world and to deliver new perspectives.

DECEMBER 24, 2011

I stared at the angel statue; her sweet, enigmatic smile had been obliterated.

"No, no, no."

The word fell in an endless string from my lips. What I saw couldn't be reality. The angel statue I had purchased—that perfect Christmas gift meant to express my deepest gratitude to my parents and the symbol of everything their support had meant to me—lay in the street. Shattered.

After hundreds of miles of transport, it had unexpectedly and tragically fallen from my trunk. All that remained was a wingless, headless torso. Jenni, my oldest daughter, broke me from my stupor.

"We can't just leave her here in the street," she said.

What else could I do? We began picking up the wreckage of the gift. With each shard scooped up and thrown into my trunk, I saw this once perfect object transformed into a hopeless pile of disconnected pieces.

The miracle of finding her had seemed divine, and I was so certain of her destiny! I was left confused and stunned. My mind retreated, and surrender opened the door.

SHATTERING: DEATH BY A THOUSAND GOOD INTENTIONS, OR DEATH BY SUCCESS

No one is immune to unexpected, life-altering events—the kind that pull the rug out from under your reality. These can leave us feeling weak, broken, worthless, terrified, fragile, and bitter. Like failures. These emotions can linger, infecting our happiest moments with self-doubt, uncertainty, and fear. Despite great comebacks, the fear of it happening again lurks subconsciously in the shadows of joy, and we build more armor to protect ourselves.

I was no stranger to shattering. My first real encounter with it almost killed me.

As a very young child, my first sincere, conscious longing came from my Catholic education. A magnet on our refrigerator read "What you are is God's gift to you. What you become is your gift to God."

I took this very seriously and literally, and I was determined to become a perfect gift for God. This became my purpose! Along the way, *becoming* somehow got confused with *achieving*.

At first, the accomplishments came effortlessly, and it was natural and fun. Then they became part of my identity: Patti the achiever. Then they became an expectation (the shoulds). Then they became the be-all and end-all for my adult life (the musts). I added being a wife, mother, and special education teacher to my list. I married my high school sweetheart, and we owned a home by the beach with our two children. I felt worthy when I was achieving. I was doing everything my religious upbringing and society confirmed was needed for a happy, successful life. Everything aligned with my ideal of perfection.

But something was missing. Deep happiness eluded me. One day a student of mine innocently asked me my favorite color. An electric shock went through me. I didn't know! I had been collecting knowledge like treasure, but I couldn't answer this simple question. I didn't know this person doing all the achieving. I felt lost and fragile.

Then, at twenty-eight, after ten years, my "perfect" marriage fell apart. The divorce was my first exposure to what felt like failure.

I fell deep into the rabbit hole of despair. In my mind, failing meant being imperfect and irreparably flawed. Feeling broken equated to being worthless, and worthless equaled hopeless. At my darkest moment, I called a crisis hotline—not because I thought I was worth saving but because I didn't want my two children to be without a mother. The human angel on the other end of the phone convinced me light remained at the end of this tunnel.

Looking back, it had never occurred to me my model of success was culturally informed and programmed and conditioned into my concept of self. I didn't realize it had nothing to do with absolute truth. Suddenly, this success formula seemed like a lie. While focusing on that distant light, I was now seeking truth.

THE "FIXING" YEARS: A SELF-IMPROVEMENT ADDICT (WITH A BIG TOOL KIT)

Shortly after the divorce, I was introduced to neurolinguistic programming (NLP), and the door opened to my first major mindset shift. I became an NLP trainer and master practitioner, and I began my pursuit of personal transformation and emotional healing.

NLP acknowledges that people are conditioned and programmed with beliefs, attitudes, and values that drive behaviors. These programs run mostly subconsciously and, once brought to consciousness, can be rewired. I was starting to see I was not my thoughts. Instead, I *had* thoughts, and when aware of these thoughts, I could change them to whatever worked better. My thoughts created my emotions, and tools and techniques existed for managing, healing from, reframing, and outright clearing negative emotions.

That old tunnel was history. I had a huge tool kit, and I headed out to relieve the world's suffering—including mine.

The greatest gifts NLP offered were the insatiable curiosity to know myself, the vigilance for uncovering clues to the subconscious, and the recognition that humans are story-making machines. (If the stories are all made up, we're free to make up good ones!)

You'd think that with this tool kit I'd have created enough armor to be and feel shatterproof. But I eventually learned this mindset only sufficed until sufficiently challenged, and being shatterproof required no armor at all.

PARADISE IS A STATE OF MIND...AND A HIGHER MIND

My NLP Master Practitioner training was in Hawaii and included an introduction to ancient Hawaiian Huna—the spiritual teachings rooted in *aloha* and a profound understanding of forgiveness called *Ho'oponopono*.

Hawaiian Huna recognizes everyone has three minds: conscious, subconscious, and higher conscious (higher self). The higher self is connected to wisdom not accessible to the conscious or rational mind, except through the subconscious channel, which is usually at capacity with thoughts, emotions, and worldly concerns. The Huna practitioner's job is to clear this channel to receive intuitive communication, guidance, and freely available wisdom. The higher self assists with forgiveness, which provides peace and harmony with others and within the self. Through years of experience, I have discovered *Ho'oponopono* can, all by itself, open this channel.

As this channel opened, I began a relationship with my HS

(higher self/Holy Spirit) that guided, comforted, and challenged me. As I grew to rely on and trust it, it blew my mind or made me laugh every day.

My personal transformation during this training redirected my entire life.

For the next fourteen years, I remained in Hawaii. I immersed myself in Hawaiian culture, danced hula, and learned from spiritual leaders. Paradise was my mindset, and I lived there. I didn't have to be perfect to live in paradise, but it seemed perfect living there. My striving for perfection was temporarily relieved.

From this state of mind, I created an international training company, offering courses in NLP, emotional management, forgiveness, and connecting to the higher self.

From this state of mind, I met a man I would marry. We combined our families and brought two daughters into the world. We bought our dream home on the Big Island.

To scale back travel, I took a corporate job, bringing the spirit of *aloha* and the guidance I was receiving into the business world. It was a rewarding time of bridging what I'd learned, inspiring others, and being financially able to help support my family. By grounding the nebulous information I'd learned firmly in the real world, I experienced firsthand that love and attention are always profitable—in business and life.

REMEMBER YOURSELF

No matter how idyllic my life, something still called me to a deeper understanding. As I became more attentive to my external life, I was also called inward. "Remember who you are and what you're here to do." This phrase repeatedly emerged in my work with others and in meditation. I was still driven to discover a truth that would resolve all conflicting spiritual teachings about who I was and why I was here. I asked life to send me a new teacher. (Oh, man! Be careful what you ask for. Life loves this request!)

Soon after, my husband returned home from lunch and handed

me *In Search of the Miraculous,* by P. D. Ouspensky. The book referenced an esoteric school initiated by G. I. Gurdjieff that continued to exist through the organization of generations of students. We tracked down a teacher from this school and began working with him via phone. After twenty-five years I continue this "work" today. Through meditation and exercises, I practice in order to "remember myself always and everywhere." This calls me into the present and my presence.

THE FIRST SHATTERED ANGEL

One day before I left for work, my six-year-old daughter crawled into my lap, begging me to stay home. We snuggled a bit. She remained insistent, but off I went. Later that morning, I received a call. She'd been hit by a truck while scootering. No amount of self-improvement had prepared me for this.

I needed a miracle.

While speeding to the hospital, I called my mentor.

"I don't know what you know that I don't know yet," I said, "but if it'll get us through this, I need you to tell me right now!"

He simply said, "Remember yourself."

I didn't eat or sleep for almost three days. I just stayed by my daughter's side and remembered myself. I shut the door to all thoughts of the ordinary mind. I willed my attention to the presence of our breathing, hers and mine. My husband joined me.

When the doctors removed her throat tube, she flatlined. I remained in peace and vigilance while my legs turned to jelly. She survived!

When she woke, she wanted to color. I walked out the door and collapsed into a coworker's arms. Her little spirit hadn't shattered. I will always remember that love and support we received from family and friends. What matters did not shatter.

You Can Take the Girl Out of Paradise, but You Can't Take Paradise Out of the Girl

When both my parents began battling cancer, we relocated to Reno, Nevada, to be closer to them and to our adult children.

We were on a new adventure! We bought a house. My husband had a great new job, and I had started a business. We were blissfully unaware the 2008 economic crash was just on the horizon.

Like dominoes, we began losing everything. My husband was laid off from his job. My business partner passed away suddenly. We lost that house, a car, and most of the business I'd started.

I felt I had failed and that my life had shattered. The most devastating part for me was asking my parents for help when they had their own hardships. I already couldn't bear their illness. I knew they were scared for themselves, and I was adding to their burden. They were gracious and without judgment, and for this I was grateful beyond comprehension.

Later, my mentor asked what I'd learned from losing everything in the economic crash.

"I learned I didn't lose myself," I said.

What matters did not shatter.

We began to rebuild. After three years of financial struggle, we got back on solid footing. We could finally afford to give my parents a Christmas gift!

I had placed so much meaning and import on this gift. When the angel shattered against the street that night, my heart broke with her.

But that ended up being the beginning of a miraculous evening that forever changed my definition of *perfection* and how I would navigate all challenges—no matter what shattered.

December 25, 2011

After the shattering came a miracle of love, faith, and focused effort. My family and I came together and meticulously glued as many of those shards together as possible. The bond of our love carried us deep into Christmas morning, taking what should have been irreparable and transforming it back into something whole. My parents had given us love, faith, and family. We, in turn, now gave them a symbol of love, faith, and family and the miracles that come from them.

A broken, shattered gift became a priceless treasure, not because she was gold but because she led us to the gold in ourselves. We, *ourselves*, are love, faith, and family! And being so, we're priceless beyond comprehension and as precious as the day we were born. The struggles and challenges just make us more precious than ever! Whatever the outcome, our efforts endow us with gifts.

MORE LESSONS FROM A "SHATTERED ANGEL"

After that night's revelations I finally understood the angel's secretive smile. She was never the real gift. The gift was what remained after the fall. These lessons I learned gave me more clarity, peace, and purpose overnight than all the previous decades of my personal development work.

"Success" is an illusion.

Success, as we typically view it, is a made-up ideal. Part of the wondrous epiphany I received with that angel gift was that you can reframe how you view success and, by extension, failure. If success isn't the goal, then there's no "failure." Failure is as much an illusion as success. If the goal is to explore, discover, and make choices, then who could fail?

Love, faith, and focused attention to any action are the ingredients for extraordinary, miraculous results.

Shattering on purpose

Anything too fixed or rigid will shatter when stressed. This applies to material objects, as well as mindsets or beliefs. One incredible gift I took from the angel experience was that shattering isn't a bad thing. Adversity is an opportunity to glimpse what really matters after devastation. Life, for the sake of goodness, will shatter our firmly held armor to answer prayers that our hearts can't even articulate.

Insight as a superpower

When things shatter, insight is the missing *peace*. When thoughts of failure and defeat creep in, I remember thoughts are just stories, and they become vapor.

When I attend beyond the words of my thinking and listen in silence, insight arrives. This is our innate superpower, inner navigation, and wisdom during any challenge. One good insight can overcome years of trying to fix what was never broken.

BEING SHATTERPROOF

Being shatterproof is who we discover we *are* as the armor of who we are *not* falls away.

When people remember the truth of who they are, struggles with doubt, fear, and self-effacement disappear. Then, you can see that you are so much more than enough! An exquisite version of love's expression. Not perfect by some made-up standard but beyond any worldly value. The very definition of *priceless*!

For much of my life, I tried to be a perfect gift for God. That ideal of perfect had to shatter to reveal this shatterproof truth.

About Patti

Patti Boes is a master practitioner and trainer in neurolinguistic programming (NLP), an interventional life coach, a forgiveness coach, an award-winning successful businesswoman, and the author of *The Shatterproof Leader: 7 Keys to Lead with Love (and Love It Too)*.

Her debut book calls for a return to love in leadership, offering a clear pathway to navigating looming challenges with greater insight, confidence, and a center of gravity that is unshakable.

Patti specializes in guiding others into expanded perspectives, new and evolving mindsets, and transformative experiences. She has spent over thirty-five years fusing teachings from modern psychology, ancient wisdom, and esoteric spirituality to quantum physics, consciousness exploration, and the reality of being, while devotedly following the questions that open and shatter fixed mindsets to unveil who we really are and our deeper purpose.

What if every day you could see doors opening to new opportunities, or feel windows opening to fresh perspectives?

What if every day you could blow your own mind with the direction a new question took you in?

Would your life be extraordinary? Could you ever stay stuck or mad or hold a grudge or stay sad?

This is Patti's passion! To throw open doors and windows and, more importantly, to create the space for friends, family, and those she works with to find the joy in this discovery.

With a compassionate voice and unwavering optimism, Patti offers you a free fifteen-minute discovery conversation.

Her upcoming projects and offerings promise to provide guidance and motivation, giving readers the tools they need to unlock their full potential and live a life of purpose and joy.

Patti's tools are not meant to fix you. You are a marvel in her eyes already. She greets you with mirrors and questions and finely tuned spectacles that expand and contract, and maybe a linguistic crowbar for heavy lifting, but mostly a large dose of faith that you can borrow, and an echo of peace of mind that is impossible to forget once you have heard it.

Patti Boes can be reached on her website or by email: www.theshatter-proofleader.com, patti@theshatterproofleader.com.

Patti lives with her husband, John, in Reno, Nevada. They have seven children and seven grandchildren, who are the joy of their world.

CHAPTER 19

DEPROGRAM TO REPROGRAM

By Kim Hattaway

WHEN THE RUBBER HITS THE ROAD

Looking at someone else's chaos can be difficult. I think of a cluttered desk and lose some confidence in that person's ability to help me do what needs to be done. Yet you see it everywhere. In the public accountant's office whose desk is a mess of client paperwork. The office at a school where everything seems to be in disarray.

I do not understand how people are able to concentrate in such a loud, chaotic environment of messiness. People talk about getting organized, but putting your life in order is not quite as easy as it might sound. There is a process that isn't always clear.

For some people, they are involved in a lifelong struggle of figuring out how to keep things together. I am not perfect. My life isn't always in order, but I have figured out the way a person goes about connecting the puzzle pieces to get to that point—a more orderly solution.

They need to have the right mindset.

One of my jobs as a Realtor is designing the best marketing plan to sell the property at top price in the least amount of time. I had a recent client whose home I was about to list. When I was able to tour the interior of the home, I was absolutely shocked at how much stuff the person had accumulated. The owners were apparently proud of their alma mater because they had paraphernalia everywhere. My jaw hit the floor. I had never seen so much of a collection. I told them the best course of action would be to depersonalize the house, which meant to take down and store everything.

The owners had to find an easy, quick solution to move and pack up their collection. Otherwise, they were running the risk of not being able to sell as quickly. How did the clients respond? At first, they were reluctant. At the end of the day, even though they were not in a rush to sell their house, they saw the light. They decided it would be best to clear the clutter out. We worked to gradually shift their mindset. If the client had not accepted my advice to declutter their home, that house may have been on the market longer than expected.

ROOTS IN ORDER

Filling my parents' shoes has been something I have strived toward throughout my entire life. We come from a small but growing town in Georgia. My father is a business owner. He has developed a variety of successful interests—along with my mother, his high school sweetheart, by his side every step of the way in his ventures. She is somewhat of a perfectionist.

My extended family has always been a very close-knit unit. Growing up in that small town, everyone tends to stay close, coming together in almost everything. Family time and operating the business can sometimes feel like one and the same. Gatherings like birthdays, holidays, barbecues, weddings, and more can become business meetings. It's just a part of who we are!

Among my father's wide range of interests is an outdoor sporting goods business. He also owns real estate interests in the area and a pecan farm, among several other companies. He is what you would refer to as an entrepreneur, a man with many connections and a big to-do list.

My mother has always supported him fullheartedly. She raised us kids, cooked supper each night, and always kept our home in perfect working order. Anytime of the day you could walk through the door into a home that felt like something out of a feature in *Southern Living* magazine. You'd never find any messes, laundry on the floor or on the bed, or dishes in the sink. Everything had a place, she had a system, and that was how things were done.

There was hardly a doubt about what I would do. I have always enjoyed working at the family business when I started answering the phones after school. Seems like a lot of responsibility to give to such a young person, especially someone just coming into middle school age. Looking at my daughter, who is a teenager now, it is hard for me to believe that I had a real job at that age.

My older siblings were always busy. They had after-school practices and activities, so my entering the working world just made sense. Working with my family was good for me. I took on that responsibility and the experience offered me some rare opportunities. Looking back, I had the chance to mature and start working on my future faster than most kids did.

Service to Others

I'm very proud of how I grew up. I like telling people that I have committed my career to helping out the family business. Working to fill my parents' shoes is a way of connecting to them. On my way up, I did other things, but my plan was always to come back to work at the family business. I wanted to help maintain the successful ventures that my parents have spent their lives building.

Working in my father's office, I learned work ethics from him, and how to make a home from my mother. That sense of order she cultivated rubbed off on me. When I was sixteen, I had the chance to take on another interesting job for some young men in their early twenties who needed housecleaning. They moved out on their own for the first time, and responsibility was something they were still working toward. They paid me to come by weekly and clean up the apartment, which was a great way to start getting in touch with the power of a clean, orderly space.

I was not just doing their dirty work. The way I looked at the job, I was helping them out. Contributing my evolving sense of order to them getting things done. From this responsibility, I learned some very valuable lessons that I still carry with me today.

Cleanliness does not just happen out of the blue. A clutter-free life is a product of intention. A person had to have the kind of mindset that prioritized taking care of those things. And there's no "clean fairy" flying around waving her magic wand, putting everything in its place after everyone goes to bed.

MAKING MY OWN WAY

Years have passed since that younger me started answering phones and cleaning up apartments. I've grown up and started a family of my own. I have always had my eye on ways to create order. When I was in college, I took a business class where I wrote an essay paper about the "paperless office" of the future. With the world becoming increasingly digital, that seemed like an appealing, realistic possibility. I was so proud of it; I still have the paper!

I have kids who struggle to maintain order, typical teenagers with their messy rooms, trash and food wrappers, clothes both clean and dirty piled up in their rooms. I ask, "Is this just a phase they are going through?" Maybe. But I know a phase, if you don't address it, can spiral out of control. Regardless, we all work together as much as we can, developing the mindset to take care of things.

That sense of direction came as part of my upbringing. I am a lot like my mother by nature, but looking back, I was not always such a neat freak. I have not always been worried about the state of things. Getting to where I am now has taken a great deal of focus and attention.

Our world is filled with distractions, especially for a person like me who struggles with attention deficit disorder, or ADD (inattentive). Sometimes when I am doing an ordinary chore, I get distracted by something like a noise in another part of the house. I have to make sure I get back to the chore I started when the interruption is completed. Sometimes I forget to complete the chore entirely. Then I come back to my bedroom after answering the phone, dealing with my kids' needs, whatever the case may be, to find the bed half-made.

I have to really work hard to focus. I create strategies. I develop little tricks just to make sure I don't lose track of what I was doing before. I create daily, weekly, and even monthly lists. Knowing what needs to get done is an invaluable part of getting there. I like to advocate for what we call the "ten-minute tidy," which is a quick rundown to straighten up right before bedtime where we pick up what does not belong and put in its place any dirty clothes or dishes, whatever the house needs. Getting the whole house in order might be overwhelming from the start, but if we can find ten minutes each day, which most of us can, the chore becomes less daunting.

Decluttering the house happens once or twice per year, usually spring and fall. I make separate piles, marking one as items to donate, another to hand down to family and friends, and one to sell; then there are those things for the trash. Everything in the home has its proper place, with no space for clutter, and the same applies on its way out. Donations and giveaways come with added benefits. Not only do they help declutter your home, but they can become a way of contributing to the community. A healthy mind creates and thrives in order.

I do not have a home out of *Southern Living* magazine, and my life is far from perfect. Few of us can make these claims. I am, however, trying to teach my children healthy organizational habits. I work with them the night before a schoolday to put their clothes out to wear, prepare their lunches, gather gym uniforms, pack book bags, charge school iPads, and more, instead of waiting until the morning, when time always seems to be tight. We also work to make sure laundry is done and put away, specifically their uniforms, so they can just put them on. Dishwasher is loaded from the day after supper, then started.

Homework is another critical point. We have to work doubly

hard to make sure they have everything that they need, books and such, in the right place with an eye on completing things on time. It's a lot of work, but it's all about mindset. Everything comes down to how a person thinks about things, figuring out what works for them, and being good to yourself.

When I think about my real estate business and clients like the one whose home was filled with paraphernalia, I think the mindset shift is a process of careful depersonalization. We all take pride in our things, especially those that we feel represent part of who we are. Our lives would ultimately be less without them, yet in the scenario where you're trying to sell your home, those personal things get in the way of what the overall objective is: selling the home for top dollar. Houses that present a relaxed, homey atmosphere allow buyers to picture themselves making the home theirs.

Selling a home comes down to being honest with people. Whether it's decor, repairs, clutter, or pricing, you need to be able to talk to them honestly about what steps they need to take. People need to hear the truth, however difficult, about what it's going to take to make the best possible sale.

WHERE TO GO FROM HERE

I have continued with my real estate career and working in the family business, running them both together while raising a young family. After all the years of walking through these doors, I am still very proud of what I have contributed.

Most know me, from my coworkers to community members to the customers who have been with us for a long time, making it so easy to be one of the local leaders for our little town. There is not much that I do not or cannot find out how to help someone with who comes to me at the store or even in town, and it feels special to be able to assist in answering questions or fill in, in a pinch. I like to think that I'll be here forever, but as I have gotten older and more mature coming into my own, I have chosen to take on other responsibilities. I have sought out the opportunity to carve something out for myself. Something that I can point to as uniquely my own, but that doesn't mean family and friends do not call or message me when they need their pantry organized or a price on a new boat or hunting land to lease. I love to help out! Even with something so seemingly simple. Helping others is my passion, especially in terms of decluttering home and office; detoxifying the body, mind, and soul; and de-stressing from outside forces of life, community, and the world for better health. Get rid of that junk that's holding you down and/or back from being the best version of yourself.

I don't know anyone who has all the time in the world. Consequently, we cannot always slow down to strategize for a more orderly, structured way of living, but when we finally do, we see that there are countless positive benefits. A home and office, even a man cave or she shed, are reflections of who we are. When we let those places get out of control, it can feel like we ourselves are out of control too. Between work and family, there is enough stress in how we live. Taking the first step in decluttering and organizing our possessions is a critical step in taking back control.

In addition, you may not realize the benefits of intermittent fasting could possibly relieve some of the health issues you may currently be experiencing. I have seen countless success stories from all over the world due to this one simple habit. Other obvious habits worth forming include proper diet, exercise, sleep, drinking lots of water, meditation, enjoying nature, and laughing, along with limiting screen time and deleting some of those "friends" in your contact list as well as on social media to reset your systems, so to speak.

Remember, you are only in competition with the person you were yesterday. We have to take care of ourselves first so we can take care of others. You won't believe how great you feel once those cluttered places are no longer there in your organized home and office, healthy mind and body, and stress-free life and community, and, of course, social media too—clear the clutter and what is not serving you best!

About Kim

Entering the workforce at an early age, Kim answered a busy, multiline phone for a boat dealership and outdoor sporting goods store. She went all the way through school and college fulfilling the duties needed to be done, from receptionist to catalog sales to secretary to office manager, with a few years farming in between harvest times, mowing and spraying herbicide strips in the many pecan orchards, until she moved away to the Atlanta area in 2000.

Shortly thereafter Kim decided to get her Real Estate Appraisers License, and in 2002 she realized "there's *no* place like home," so she took her career to the next level and jumped into the highly competitive world of residential sales and moved back to her hometown of Perry! Kim and her partner began land clearing and development LLCs, new construction homes, and land/lot investments, but real estate sales was her passion.

Kim, being highly determined, quickly learned competitive tactics from the best in the biz. She built a successful real estate team and won many awards assisting hundreds of families with achieving their goals of buying and selling property. Kim founded her own real estate brokerage, Real Estate Insider, in 2009, a company that provides a menu of services to fit any budget because no home or client is the same.

In 2024 Kim is back better than ever with her husband by her side, concentrating on her growing hometown of Perry and her community to give back strong! They, along with their teenagers, are building a family-oriented team to help cover all facets of the preparation for their clients. Her mission is to maximize the value that she brings to them. She has strategic plans backed by market research to give sellers a maximized return on their investment and to help buyers find the perfect home, always negotiated at the best price. Kim is all about simplicity—health, wealth, and happier living! She truly is all about decluttering the home, detoxifying the mind, and de-stressing from outside forces.

Affiliated with NAR, GAR, CGAR, Central Georgia MLS, the Perry Chamber of Commerce, the Perry Board of Realtors, CrossPoint Baptist Church of Perry, Perry local schools, the National Academy of Best-Selling Authors, America's PremierExperts, and the National Association of Expert Advisors Commitment to Excellence Awards, she appeared on *The New Masters of Real Estate* TV show, seen on NBC, ABC, CBS, and FOX affiliates around the country!

- Kim Hattaway, Real Estate Insider
- (478) 256-0136 (Call/Text#)
- HattawayGirl@gmail.com
- www.Facebook.com/HattawayGirl2022
- Search Homes instantly at www.GetKAT.com.
- TikTok: www.tiktok.com/@HattawayHealth
- "One sip closer to better health": https://ufeelgreat.com/c/XLD338

CHAPTER 20

LIGHT ME UP

By Victoria Rader

In the rich, complex mosaic of my childhood, set against the stark, gray canvas of Ukraine under the Soviet regime, my formative years were intricately shaped by the dual presence of tradition and resilience. Amid this backdrop, marked by a somber palette of societal restrictions, my early years blossomed under the nurturing watch of my grandparents. My parents, immersed in the relentless tides of their professional pursuits, alternated my care between my two sets of grandparents, who embodied the enduring spirit of our homeland. This environment, a peculiar blend of security and constriction, served as both cradle and crucible, nurturing my nascent spirit while igniting the flames of curiosity and imagination within me.

It is within this context that a memory, vivid and profound, emerges from the depths of my past, casting long shadows over the landscape of my memories. I was but five years old, enveloped in the innocence and wonder of childhood, when a day of simple play transformed into a moment of unexpected awakening. Under the vigilant eyes of my grandfather Volodya, a figure of control and strength and wisdom, I found myself lost in the world of make-believe and adventure. It was during this play that I, in a burst of childlike innovation, repurposed a seemingly harmless object—a metal pin, plucked from the tangled locks of my hair— into a makeshift hook for my doll's dress.

Driven by a creative spark, I approached the wall socket, an ordinary fixture in our modest home, chosen as the stage for my doll's new wardrobe. Unaware of the latent dangers lurking within, I proceeded with the innocence of youth, guided by imagination rather than caution. The act of inserting the metal pin into the socket, pure though it was, set off a chain of events that would leave an indelible mark on my young mind.

The moment the pin touched the heart of the socket, the house was plunged into silence and darkness—a protective measure, as the household fuse, acting as a silent sentinel, ceased the flow of electricity, averting what could have been a catastrophic event. The air, charged with a mix of fear and confusion, became the backdrop for a lesson in energy and safety that I would carry with me for the rest of my life.

This seemingly minor event in the grand tapestry of life later blossomed into a profound metaphor that I would weave into my teachings. It highlighted the delicate balance between risk and safety, the thin line that separates curiosity from recklessness. The blown fuse, in its silent sacrifice, mirrored the safeguards we unknowingly erect against the currents of life.

In the aftermath of the incident, my grandfather Volodya, his face a complex tapestry of anger and relief, fear and stern concern, ran into the room and knelt beside me. His voice, usually calm and steady, carried a tremor of urgency and poorly suppressed anger, as he attempted to explain the dangers of my action. "You could have died," he said, his eyes locking with mine. "What you did was very dangerous." He was conveying to me that we must respect the energy that powers our lives, just as we respect the force of a storm or the flow of a river. His words carried the weight of his fears as a reflection of the depth of his love.

Through this experience, and the wisdom imparted by my grandfather, I began to understand the unseen forces that govern our world. The electricity that flowed through our home, invisible yet omnipresent, became a symbol of life's hidden energies. In Ukraine, where the very air seemed charged with unspoken stories of survival and resistance, I learned that the forces shaping our existence are often beyond our sight but not beyond our influence.

The lesson of the blown fuse, a silent guardian against the surge of untamed energy, illuminated a vital truth: Just as a home is filled with a constant flow of electricity, our lives are permeated by a continuous stream of energy. This energy, boundless and indifferent, offers itself to us in every moment. Yet it is not the sheer force of this energy that defines the brightness of our existence; rather, it is our own resistance, our internal settings, that determine the intensity of the light we cast into the world.

This understanding, born from a moment of childhood curiosity and the wise words of a loving grandfather, became a cornerstone of my worldview. It taught me that while we may not control the vast energies of life, we possess the power to channel, shape, and temper them through the lens of our own spirit. This realization, a blend of my grandfather's wisdom and the indelible experiences of my youth, forged the foundation of my journey from a curious child playing in the shadow of the Soviet era to a teacher and guide, seeking to illuminate the unseen pathways of the human heart.

This profound realization, unearthed from the depths of childhood memory, became the bedrock of my philosophical journey, casting light on the intricate dance between our innermost fears and the radiant essence we all possess. The paradox is as poignant as it is perplexing: Our very defenses, the barriers we erect in the name of self-preservation, often cast the longest shadows, dimming the brilliance we yearn to express. Why, then, do we retreat into the comforting embrace of darkness, ensnared by the chains of our own making? The roots of this enigma stretch deep, intertwined with the primal mechanisms of survival, much like the safety fuse that played its silent, protective role in the narrative of my youth. These mechanisms, while originally designed as guardians of our well-being, can inadvertently morph into the very walls that confine us, a gilded cage restricting us to the realm of existence, far removed from the luminous potential of true living.

The events of that fateful day, the electric spark of danger met with the protective clutch of a fuse, transcend the mere boundaries of childhood whimsy. They weave their threads through the very fabric of my existence, mirroring the broader tapestry of human struggle and aspiration. In the aftermath my grandfather's words, heavy with concern and cold in their delivery, did more than merely alert me to the peril I had narrowly escaped. They ignited the first sparks of an ongoing internal conflict, a relentless tug-of-war between the innate drive to discover, to push beyond the known, and the deep-seated impulse to seek refuge, to safeguard the sanctity of life.

This internal struggle, this dance between curiosity and caution, found new resonance and depth in the face of a haunting episode beside the Black Sea. A family excursion, painted with the hues of innocence and the tranquil beauty of nature, was dramatically transformed into an arena of stark reality as we stumbled upon the desperate efforts to revive Valera, a young man swallowed by the sea's unforgiving embrace. This moment, frozen in time, became a stark memento of life's fragile balance, etching a profound lesson into my young heart and mind. The relentless waves, indifferent in their might, whispered harsh truths about the precarious nature of existence, sewing seeds of a deep-seated fear of water, a symbol now laden with the somber weight of mortality.

This episode, a stark confrontation with the raw, unfiltered edges of life, cast long, indelible shadows over the landscape of my youth. It was more than a lesson in the physical perils that lurk in the world's hidden corners; it was a metaphorical crossing into a world where caution shapes every step, where every decision is tinged with the memory of what might lie beneath the tranquil surface. The somber hues of these early experiences colored my approach to life's vast, unpredictable waters, instilling a cautiousness that extended far beyond the tangible realm of physical safety.

This cautiousness, born from the trials and tribulations of early encounters with life's capricious nature, evolved into a broader, more encompassing metaphor. It became emblematic of the emotional and psychological fortifications we construct in our quest to navigate the unpredictable currents of existence. These barriers, while serving as bulwarks against the tide of uncertainties, also stand as silent sentinels, reminders of the delicate balance we must strike. They symbolize the perpetual battle between the desire to leap into the unknown, to explore the boundless potential that lies beyond the familiar, and the instinctual need to retreat, to seek solace in the safety of known harbors.

Thus, my journey, marked by moments of revelation and reflection, continues to be shaped by the interplay of light and shadow, of daring and caution. The narrative of my life, from the carefree days of childhood to the reflective passages of adulthood, is a testament to the enduring struggle between the essence of who we might become and the protective layers we wrap around our core. It is a journey marked by the continual quest to find balance, to navigate the intricate pathways between the sanctuaries of safety and the vast, uncharted territories of potential that await beyond the fortress of our fears.

As time unfolded, my life's narrative was marked by oscillations between exhilaration and melancholy. Particularly the year 2013 stands etched in my memory, a time shadowed by the departure of dear ones, leaving an indelible mark on my essence. In one year I lost eleven people I was close to, with a mechanical prediction of one leaving this mortal realm every month due to diverse causes. This epoch, intertwined with personal upheavals and professional challenges, morphed into a chrysalis from which a new perspective emerged. External achievements of my best year in real estate, collecting accolades as the 1 percent agent in the US, seemed hollow against the backdrop of inner turmoil, grief, and despair, catalyzing a profound reevaluation of my direction and purpose.

In this abyss a glimmer of understanding pierced the enveloping darkness—a serene yet assertive voice of inner wisdom, which I recognized as Spirit. It offered a luminary of hope in the dense fog of my despair. The message it bore was succinct yet transformative: The path from obscurity to enlightenment is illuminated not by chasing the darkness away but by turning on the light. This insight, though elemental, revolutionized my entire being, heralding a fresh beginning.

This awakening spurred the creation of YU2SHINE, a venture born out of a fervent desire to distill and disseminate the enlightenment I had stumbled upon. It emerged as a beacon for those meandering through the complexities of life, aiming to light up paths with the lessons carved from my personal odyssey. YU2SHINE's mission is predicated on a simple yet profound belief: Within each person lies an untapped brilliance, a beacon of light capable of not just personal transformation but also of casting ripples across the global canvas.

At the heart of this mission lies the conviction that our mindset—our constructed realities, beliefs, and attitudes—holds the compass to our life's direction. The intricate dance of our mental faculties—perception, imagination, intuition, reason, memory, and will—crafts the mosaic of our existence. By aligning and fine-tuning these faculties toward a unified vision, we transition from the penumbral margins of mere existence to the vibrant core of authentic living.

Our life stories, woven from threads of varying hues—joy, despair, victories, and setbacks—present a kaleidoscope of experiences. Within this intricate web, we face the constant interplay of our dual selves: the scared self, or "scared me," of "little m," "mortal matter manifesting materially," a persona shackled by fears and transience, and the Sacred mE, "big E," Eternal Energy Expanding our boundless, radiant Essence. This internal dichotomy is the battleground of our souls, where the deepest conflicts and the most luminous revelations unfold.

The quest for enlightenment, for the full embodiment of our "big E," resembles a voyage through an uncharted wilderness. In my own journey, the law of trust has been a steadfast guide. This principle asserts that the most profound guidance is not found in the external chaos but springs from the quiet depths of our inner wisdom. By heeding this internal guide, even amid life's tempests, we uncover paths laden with unexpected treasures and transformative truths.

YU2SHINE stands as a sentinel on this journey, providing a constellation of tools, resources, and wisdom to aid seekers in discovering their intrinsic luminescence. Whether it's through the practical steps outlined in the Empower-mE app, the profound insights shared in Prosper mE, or the tailored guidance offered in our workshops, the aim remains unwavering: to embolden individuals to tread their paths with fortitude, clarity, and a profound commitment to their personal evolution.

As you set forth on this pilgrimage, bear in mind that the illumination you seek dwells not in the distant beyond but within the sanctum of your own spirit. Embracing this inner flame, peeling away the veils of doubt and apprehension, represents the most pivotal journey of your existence. It's a passage from the shadowed realm of the "scared me" to the luminous expanse of the "Sacred mE," a transition from the constraints of mere survival to the expansive freedom of flourishing.

Thus, I extend an invitation to you: Dive deep into the narrative of your life, confront the challenges, wrestle with the uncertainties, and revel in the moments of joy. Perceive these experiences not as deterrents but as catalysts propelling you toward growth and self-realization. The world, in all its multifaceted splendor, awaits the unique brilliance that only you can contribute. It's time to stride forth, to radiate your light, to unfurl the vast potential of your "big E."

Embark on this journey; forge your trail. Let the beacon of your inner light steer your course. Embrace your radiant self, for the universe yearns for the singular splendor only you are capable of bestowing.

Be you! All of you are born to be! Light mE Up!

About Victoria

Victoria Rader, Possibility Coach® and founder of YU2SHINE, is a globally known transformational speaker and a pioneer of Quantum Personal Development. She stands as a transformative force in the realm of spiritual and personal growth. With an unparalleled blend of wisdom drawn from the depths of metaphysical study and an innate understanding of the human spirit, Victoria has crafted a legacy that bridges the tangible with the mystical, guiding individuals to the precipice of their potential and beyond.

Her academic prowess is underscored by a PhD in metaphysical studies, augmenting her spiritual teachings with robust intellectual underpinnings. As a pioneering creator of the Master-mE and Empower-mE Apps and the innovative Quantum Freedom™ and Free mE EFT™ techniques, she has seamlessly integrated technology and ancient wisdom, offering tools for healing and empowerment at the fingertips of those she serves.

As a multiple-time international best-selling author, her literary contributions offer a compass for navigating life's tumultuous seas, guiding readers to the shores of financial freedom and spiritual abundance. From the award-winning *Prosper mE* book to *mE* journals and a star of the *Zero Limits Living* movie, her voice, a harmonious blend of authority and compassion, resonates within the inner truth of her readers, viewers, audiences, and clients alike, leaving indelible marks on their hearts and minds.

Victoria is also renowned and awarded for her Abundant mE teachings of how one's mindset is harmonized via mastery of six mental faculties and their corresponding universal laws. Victoria's life is a testament to the philosophy that everything is possible when aligned with LOVE—life originating vibrant emotion (energy in motion). Her mission, articulated through YU2SHINE, is to ignite the sacred flame within each individual, empowering them to dismantle the barriers of the "little m" and embrace the limitless expanse of their "big E": mortal surrendering to Eternal, matter to Energy, manifesting to Expanding, and material to Essential.

Victoria is deeply grateful to her family for all the love and support. They remain her greatest why.

Join Victoria Rader on a journey not just of self-discovery but of universal rediscovery, where each step forward is a step into the infinite possibilities of your truest self.

To start your journey, visit Scared me to Sacred mE at www. ChooseSacred.mE, and connect with Victoria: IG @vica_rader, www. yu2shine.com.

CHAPTER 21

A TALE OF TWO MINDSETS

By Pritesh Lohar, MD, FACP

"For each weakness there is a corresponding strength."
—ROBERT GREENE, *THE LAWS OF HUMAN NATURE*

As I bask in the sunshine—literally and figuratively—lounging on a Sunday morning in my penthouse suite in India, I am reflecting and reliving the events that got me here.

There is no doubt that our mindset is what determines our ability to grow and succeed. I am eager to talk about my current mindset, but before I share, it's important to understand that there comes a time in our lives when one cannot hide the thoughts, memories, and emotions buried deep within us. Through that empowering insight, I gained the power to transform old trauma into a healing mindset.

Be forewarned. It's one filled with pain and shame and things I am not proud of.

My childhood was filled with contradictions and dysfunction. The one thing that stood out in my childhood was a mindset of lack. Other negative factors started to creep in—fear, hate, shame, guilt, worry, anxiety, insecurity, inferiority, and so on.

The dysfunction and isolation were so bad, fantasy was my only solace. And from there started my life full of addictions, living a dual life, desperate to hide my behaviour, and at the same time wanting to act out.

———•———

The first serious failure in my life happened when I was twenty-seven, and since then there have been several major failures/rejections/disappointments. So what is it about mindset, and success and failure?

I started to struggle with studies and work in my early twenties. I started my medical residency back in 1989. Within a couple of weeks of my joining, I was left to work independently, as would be the norm. I had sixty admissions on my first outpatient day and felt so overwhelmed.

Instead of asking for help, I ran away from work. It was one of the lowest points of my life. I was trained from childhood to not ask for help, and that cost me a lot in life, as the pattern continued. My fixed mindset had me believe all the time, "I can't do this," instead of, "I can't do this yet."

I judged myself and others quite harshly, with no compassion, eventually leading me to a victim mindset. Whenever I was rejected in various areas of life, I felt judged critically, and found I was loving myself even less. Every criticism was deemed by me as a flaw of my character. I don't think I learned much from any negative experience; if anything, it made me more bitter and vengeful.

My dysfunctions were masked or ignored by me in India, largely because of the social culture. But my thoughts were so different from reality. After I started working in the US in 1996, I met my ex-wife, a year later in 1997. I admired her and was attracted to her. We dated for about eight months. I felt I genuinely loved her, and we decided to get married in 1998.

———•———

The following nine years were right out of a Hollywood movie. Carol Dweck has written an entire chapter on the "Mindsets in Love" (or not). As she writes in her book, "With the fixed mindset, one moment your partner is the light of your life, the next they

214

are your adversary. In the fixed mindset, there are only 2 choices, blame your own permanent qualities or blame your partner's." I don't think most people would have to guess which way I went. Communication between the two of us was minimal, leading to several misunderstandings and assumptions. Mind reading would inevitably backfire.

For the first time in my life I discovered that I had a dysfunction, which needed to be addressed emotionally and spiritually. We went to individual therapy, marital counseling, and other couple's therapy. But the continual emotional and verbal hurt given out to each other and indulging in blame games did not help. The only things holding us together were our two boys.

In December 2005, while on Christmas break in Orlando, I stayed confined to my small room, watching *The Lord of The Rings* movies, while she was in another bedroom with the boys. As I lay down to sleep, I seemed to find no answer as to how things would get any better and remained defeated. I felt bad for the boys, for them to be witness to all the shouting and screaming. The universe was listening. Six months later, in July 2006, my roller coaster of a life started.

I craved for relationships and connections out of marriage, and that's where my dysfunctions, addictions and saboteurs took over. Three distinct events happened over a span of fifteen years, which finally made me realize I was the problem, and not the world. Each time the pattern was the same.

———•———

While working in Ontario, Canada, in 2006, I started texting and emailing my secretary, and she reciprocated well even though she was married. As soon as her husband found out, she accused me of pursuing her.

I left that job and started working in Saskatchewan in 2007. A nurse was assigned to me, and we got friendly. I told her about the things I had gone through in my previous job, and she first told the administration about it, who then exhorted her to file a complaint against me.

Since I was in my initial one-year probationary period, they fired me without due process. These two events in less than a year filled me with guilt and shame, enough to make me contemplate suicide by jumping in the icy-cold waters of the Saskatchewan River. But I didn't.

I went to court, and after nine months of not working, I was running out of funds and in danger of filing bankruptcy. Besides, with my work visa coming to an end, I could no longer live there.

I returned home to India, having lost my family, job, money, and reputation. My ex-wife and I got legally separated, as she took the boys to the US.

After returning to India, I started working again. The previous experiences had sobered me up a bit, but within four to five years my triggers were starting to act up. Sometimes subconsciously and sometimes consciously, I found myself walking in the old way. Drinking alcohol would just make the situation worse.

———•———

As I got busier, accepting more responsibilities, I found myself reaching out to women indiscriminately, thinking they could fill the emptiness inside me. Somehow I knew I was walking down the wrong path again, and while the consequences scared me, it's as if I didn't expect anything to happen.

As it turned out, none of the females were serious; most of them were only planning to use me. While at work I tried to stay away from other doctors and administration personnel who themselves were in this behavior, but it was difficult.

The final episode of this gruesome chapter took me back to practice in the US again in 2020. It was a small town, I was isolated, with no friends, and there was plenty of snow. I wasn't enjoying my job at all. On top of that COVID was hitting everyone around me hard.

A hospital pharmacist, who was undergoing a divorce, became my next friend, but only on the condition that I should communicate with her through the hospital system with messaging. She wanted communication between us a total secret, and my dysfunction was to the fore because while knowing it was all wrong, I decided to go along with her wishes.

I really thought she was the one for me. However, after revealing quite a few details about her family, soon to be "ex-husband," and various other things, she started to become paranoid.

She accused me of stalking her and eventually filed a complaint. I left my job abruptly, knowing I could never justify my communication at work with her. She, on the other hand, was put on administrative leave and then released. But the story didn't end there.

She had me under surveillance and sent notices through her lawyer for extortion. All this stress had my BP going to very high levels, requiring three hospital admissions in a week, the last of which happened on the day I was supposed to be in court for my first divorce hearing and the packers were coming in to move my household goods internationally.

For those of you familiar with *The Monk Who Sold His Ferrari*, by Robin Sharma, it just about sums up my story, like Julian on the floor.

As I sat in silence inside my dark house, locked and bolted, I asked myself the question "How do I get into these situations without any malicious intent? Was I just unlucky?" Likely not.

The law of attraction states that like *attracts* like. I attracted what my energy vibrated.

The law of vibration states that human thoughts, feelings, and physical bodies also vibrate at higher frequencies, and this vibration influences our reality and interactions. I could have attracted positive experiences and outcomes into my life had I been cognizant of that.

The law of correspondence is the most interesting. It states that patterns repeat throughout the universe (familiar to me), and that the microcosm reflects the macrocosm. On a personal level it suggested that by aligning my personal frequency with higher frequencies, I could achieve a state that mirrored the harmony and balance seen in the larger universe. This motivated me to align my inner state with my outer state.

———•———

The law of perpetual transmutation of energy suggests that individuals have the power to change the condition of their lives by transforming their personal energy or vibration. Higher frequencies have the power to transform lower vibrations, leading to positive changes. This was the game changer for me.

I happened to read in a book somewhere, "Evolution is ruthless and unforgiving—it doesn't teach by showing you what works but by destroying what doesn't." Hard, hard truth. It was about that time that I realized I had to evolve into my higher self. There is always a higher lesson and a deeper message from the universe.

I thought of my boys and my parents and concluded this is not the legacy I wanted to leave behind. My main fixed mindset trigger was failure. Now, after having failed so many times in my life in examinations, relationships, expectations, and many more, I concluded that changing my way of thinking was the only way I could change my life. I could not do the same way of thinking and living and expect a different result.

While I didn't even read about the Satir Model of change, things just about went that way for me. It was here that science met my spirit, even though change is never easy.

There was this *late status quo*, for a few months leading to May 2022, where things just didn't seem right. I could sense something was about to shift and felt uneasy. It felt as if a spiritual attack was happening. First, I happened to have a bad case of laryngopharyngeal reflux; then I hit myself in my groin area (accidentally) with a wooden hanger, and I failed my recertification exams.

———i———

Then happened the state of *resistance*, where the external events triggered my internal realization. I was fearful in some ways of giving up the familiar and altering established patterns. This resistance created quite a bit of conflict within me. In short I wanted to become a good person without giving up the old habits.

The third phase became *chaos*, as old patterns started to break down without new ones to replace them. I feared returning to the old ways. This stage was marked by confusion, emotional upheaval, and a sense of being lost. But looking back, I find it was where I had the greatest potential for growth.

This led to *integration*, where through exploration and experimentation, new options and behaviors were discovered, tested, and integrated. This began to feel like renewal and transformation.

Finally, the *new status quo* was formed, with increased self-esteem and confidence, as I successfully navigated the change process and emerged stronger.

The good thing about mindsets is that everybody has both mindsets. The first step toward growth was acceptance of my fixed mindset, just like I accepted my dark parts. The challenge initially was to accept how frequently it would show up and how much damage it could cause.

The next step was to recognize my fixed-mindset triggers—it's like a saboteur telling you to do unwise things. The triggers could be a failure, a rejection, knowing somebody has achieved something significant, thereby inviting thoughts of jealousy and envy, facing overwhelming challenges, or facing criticism, thereby making me more judgmental.

———i———

The resilience I had gained through these struggles restored my balance. I remained assured that I held enough power to create monumental change.

Everything that has happened in my life has been by divine order. I now understand how each trial, each test, each relationship, and each triumph was aligned for my highest self. I am finding peace with my past and surrendering to the mystery of the future.

The key is to live fully in each present moment so I can unlock my blissful life. Nowadays I watch whom I give my energy to. I have learned to cut off people from my life who were draining me.

Transitioning from a fixed mindset to a growth mindset was challenging, requiring consistent effort and practice. I had assumed that my character, intelligence, and creative abilities were static and could not be changed in a meaningful way. As it turned out, this was one of my biggest self-limiting beliefs.

I could now see failure not as evidence of unintelligence but as a springboard for growth and stretching my existing abilities to thrive on challenges.

This was very hard (and still is), but instead of taking criticism personally, I use it as feedback to improve. I began to appreciate the role of effort in mastering a new skill and knowledge area, in this case personal transformation and coaching others.

———◦———

Instead of feeling threatened by the success of others, I began to celebrate their achievements and learn from their experiences. I began to change my self-talk, focusing on the language I use with myself. Practicing mindfulness and reflection reinforced my shift toward a growth mindset.

The law of oneness is based on the belief that everything in the universe is connected and part of a single, infinite energy field. It meant that by raising my frequency, I could not only improve my own life but also contribute to the upliftment of the collective consciousness. This is in alignment with my current life purpose of coaching for improvement.

While I achieved a lot, even with my fixed mindset, there

lingers the feeling that I could have fulfilled my full potential with embracing a growth mindset earlier.

But I can say, with God's help and without hubris, that I'm now becoming a pretty good person.

About Dr. Lohar

Pritesh Lohar, MD, FACP, is a board-certified medical oncologist and hematologist. While successfully treating cancer patients for two decades, he finally found his life purpose and passion: being a life coach, changing limiting beliefs and upleveling the mindset of his clients for personal and business growth and expansion is his mission.

While performing his clinical duties, he successfully became certified as a life coach and 6-Phase meditation trainer by Mindvalley. Additionally, he is certified in Daniel Goleman's Foundational and Relational Skills of Emotional Intelligence.

He is currently pursuing International Coaching Federation (ICF) credentialing and certification as a Professional Certified Coach (PCC). His areas of expertise and interest include mindset and high-performance coaching. He is also recognized as an artificial intelligence transformation officer, having completed the AI Mastery course by Mindvalley.

Dr. Lohar is the founder and CEO of The School of Mindset Coaching and Coach NextGen, concentrating primarily on mindset and transformational coaching and business coaching. Earlier this year he was honored as one of the Achievers of Asia & Africa 2024 by *Passion Vista* magazine.

His approach to coaching is based on a foundation of empathy, active listening, and nonjudgment. He believes that everyone has unique talents waiting to be unleashed, and he is here to support and guide them in realizing their dreams and aspirations.

Through personalized coaching sessions, he helps individuals cultivate self-confidence, enhance their communication skills, improve decision-making abilities, and create balance in various aspects of their lives. He focuses on areas such as self-awareness, goal setting, mindset shifts, and developing effective strategies to overcome obstacles.

His dedication, passion, and unwavering belief in the potential of others have transformed countless lives. Through his relentless pursuit of personal growth and his commitment to empowering others, Dr. Lohar exemplifies the transformative power of coaching and serves as an inspiration for anyone seeking to make a difference in the world.

Dr. Lohar's goal is to impact as many lives positively as he can by imparting his coaching skills and life experiences to others. His life experiences have taught him that "life is happening for me," and he believes imparting that experience and belief with as many individuals as possible is beneficial to humanity.

When not working, he spends time with his parents in India or with his two boys in the USA and traveling around the world.

CONNECT WITH DR. LOHAR:

https://www.schoolofmindsetcoaching.com
https://www.coachnextgen.com

CHAPTER 22

IT'S NEVER TOO LATE TO REWRITE YOUR STORY

By John Mitchell

I can still feel the perspiration on my forehead and the back of my neck. I can still feel the aches in my lower back, my legs, even my feet.

I also can still remember my weight. I was 370 pounds. I had gotten there the way everyone else gets there—through a combination of unhealthy eating habits, a lack of exercise, and a sedentary lifestyle. Too many desserts. Too many sodas. Too many portions. Too much time in my car, in my office, on my couch. Too little time on my feet.

It seemed like an unbreakable cycle, and my health was paying the price.

Climbing a flight of stairs was a daunting task. So was tying my shoes. And taking a long walk. And boarding a commercial airline—its seats uncomfortably small, uncomfortably too close to the next passenger. I particularly remember the dread knowing I would have to push the overhead call button and ask for an extension for the seat belt that was never quite long enough to encompass my considerable girth—and the disapproving stares of the passengers around me. My weight affected my emotional and mental health too—a constant reminder of my limitations, a constant reminder that there were certain tasks in life I just couldn't do.

Of course, weight loss doesn't happen overnight. Neither does success. Both take determination. Both take perseverance.

At the time, my wife and I were in our forties and running a consumer finance business in Guadalajara, Mexico, having moved there on a whim—we are from the US but enjoy adventure and travel—and having secured a nice lifestyle with a career in the financial sector. Like a sailboat on a strategic course, we had gotten there with hard work and lots of planning. We were, to put it mildly, in calm waters. But unlike the crew of that sailboat, I was wanting a more challenging course in life, filled with unknowns. I was wanting a new career.

I guess you can blame Perry Mason. As an eight-year-old boy growing up in Arkansas, I would watch that classic black-and-white drama, cheering on America's favorite criminal defense attorney as he skillfully defended his clients in the courtroom. He was the smartest guy on television. (After all, he had a library of a thousand books!) He was the wisest one too. (In 271 episodes over nine seasons, he lost only one case). Most importantly, Perry Mason defended the little guy. He stood up for justice. He wasn't afraid to stand in for David and take on Goliath.

"I want to be a lawyer," I told my schoolmates.

But that dream took a three-decade detour when I developed an interest in finance. I was a tax professional for much of my life, busting my butt from January through April—one-hundred-hour weeks, fueled by caffeine and sugar—and then mostly coasting through the other eight months as I engaged in side projects for fun, every year waiting for January so I could start it all over again. All along, though, the dream of being an attorney was in the back of my mind. I wanted to take up for David against Goliath, and I wanted to win.

Fortunately, my new home city of Guadalajara had a law school a mere eight blocks from my home. Even better, it offered night classes. I could continue my work in the financial industry during daytime hours to pay the bills, and I could chase my legal dreams at night as I pursued my law degree—all at the age of forty-two.

That's where I was that evening as I wiped away the perspiration.

That's where I was as I tried to ignore the aches and pains in my back, legs, and feet.

I was determined to earn my law degree. I was just as determined to lose weight. As they say back in Arkansas, I was on a hunt to "kill two birds with one stone." I dropped sodas from my diet. I cut out sweets. I lowered my portion sizes. Just as important, I started exercising.

From day one of law school, I chose to walk—not drive—to class. The eight-block trek took about thirty minutes each way, giving me an hour's worth of daily exercise and—including the remainder of my day—about ten thousand daily steps.

It wasn't easy. The first few days, I arrived at class slightly winded and not so slightly wet. It didn't help that I was carrying a ten-pound bag with books, folders, and other essentials. It also didn't help that the temperature was often warm. Soon, though, the route became easier, and as weeks turned to months, I was making the walk with ease, enjoying the sights, scents, and sounds of Guadalajara—the scents from open-air restaurants, the sounds of lively music, the beauty of historical, centuries-old buildings—as I made the daily sixteen-block round trip.

I graduated three years later, thus launching my career as a tax attorney.

I also lost 150 pounds.

It was a turning point in my life—a life that has been filled with firsts. Already, I was the first member of my family to attend college and to graduate from college. Now, I was the first member of my family to earn a law degree. Later, I added a master's degree. And I did it with honors, graduating as the class valedictorian in law school and earning a 4.0 in my master's classes—proving that it's never too late for a middle-aged, forty-something guy to start over in life. As I've learned, it's also never too late to chase your dreams.

Three simple maxims have helped me succeed: (1) Don't be afraid, (2) take a bold step forward, and (3) persevere.

After all, I had plenty of reasons not to try: I was an

English-speaking overweight guy living in a Spanish-speaking country where my skin color—I'm Caucasian—stood out wherever I went. I had excuses galore: *I'm too old. I'm too lazy. I'm not smart enough. Besides, the language barrier is just too difficult! I won't understand my professors. They won't understand me.*

To be honest, all those excuses swirled around in my head that first month as I enrolled in a major degree program for the first time in a couple of decades, my heart racing. My heart pounded fast again as I walked through the door for class on that first day, my professor greeting us with a smile and a friendly "*¡Buenas noches!*" as he proceeded to use a few unfamiliar words I had yet to learn. I smiled back and took notes, determined to make it to the end. Much like that sailboat on rough waters, I was intent on navigating through the unknown and reaching my destination.

Fast-forward to today.

As a tax attorney for Cantrell & Cantrell, based in Houston, I have the privilege of being the "Perry Mason" for clients who, to put it mildly, are stuck in life's proverbial ditch. Any of us could end up there, thanks in part to a confusing mesh of tax laws that can tangle anyone in their web. (Albert Einstein, who developed the mind-bending theory of relativity, famously told his accountant, "The hardest thing in the world to understand is the income tax.")

Yes, there are indeed individuals who intentionally flout the tax law and then pray they never get caught. Often, though, the IRS targets people on the lower end of the financial classes who don't even realize they might be violating the law. And sometimes the IRS targets people who are flat-out innocent.

"When I talk to you, I feel better," one of my clients recently said.

I hear that a lot. When you're a "little guy" and you open a letter from the IRS, it's easy to feel as if you're in an unwinnable battle. My job is to calm their nerves, represent their side, and find a few smooth stones.

One time the administrator of a home health care company

phoned my office, his voice filled with fear and his legal case sounding, at first, daunting.

"The IRS has fined us two million dollars," he said pessimistically. "I've read the law—we indeed broke it."

The details of the case, though, gave us a fighting chance. The IRS brought the case in the early days of the Affordable Care Act (Obamacare), a then new US law that provided health insurance to millions of people who previously had none. That same law, though, came with plenty of red tape for employers. The problem? The company's previous owner, a sweet seventy-something woman with a big heart and good intentions, knew little of the law's requirements. Each violation came with a fine of hundreds of dollars. And with six hundred–plus employees, the company was, technically, guilty of a few thousand violations. When she died of cancer, it muddied the legal landscape even more. Not a single penny of tax had gone unpaid. The company was providing health insurance that met all the requirements to its employees. Its sole sin was that it did not fill out the thousands of pages of paperwork to report it all to the government.

The IRS fines would have impacted not only hundreds of employees but thousands of innocent sick people too. Unfortunately, the company didn't have the money to pay up.

After spending hours upon hours reading the law, I made my case to a hearing officer at the IRS Independent Office of Appeals.

"Yes, the IRS could fine this company," I told him, "but you're going to put this company out of business. And because of that, not only will these hundreds of people lose their livelihoods, but sick people throughout this community are going to be without health care services. Quite frankly—and I'm not exaggerating here—someone could die."

I continued: "The IRS can fine this company, but you'll eventually be on the six o'clock news for causing the death of an innocent elderly person."

I walked out of the hearing knowing I was right, even if the IRS stubbornly stood its ground. Maybe that was my Perry Mason moment. I prefer to call it common sense. Within days the IRS agreed to drop the fines. My client was elated.

Another time, a woman called me, her voice sounding defeated.

"I'm facing three million dollars in IRS penalties," she said.

At first, her case seemed even more formidable than the first one. The IRS was charging her with willful failure of her reporting requirements after she ran companies on both sides of the border—in both the US and Mexico—without filing the necessary financial disclosures. Even worse, she was an attorney in Mexico.

I still remember the words of the IRS agent: "She's no innocent party. She knew the law."

But once I dug a little deeper, I learned she indeed *was* innocent. She didn't have access from her business partner to the company financial records that were necessary for her to file the proper paperwork. In other words, it was materially impossible for her to follow the law. You can't file a report when you don't have access to the documents. In technical terms, we'd call her an "innocent spouse."

The IRS dropped the fines.

Still another time, a man phoned me, struggling for words as he explained that he operated a nonprofit organization that assisted immigrants.

"We just received a long, threatening letter from the IRS," he said, panicked. "They say we lost our nonprofit status six years ago."

Without that nonprofit status, his organization would have owed millions of dollars in back taxes and fines—and likely would have ceased to exist. No doubt, countless immigrants would have suffered.

We won that case too. The nonprofit status was reinstated. Retroactively.

The work of a tax attorney often involves hours and hours of drudgery—hours upon hours of reviewing complex tax codes, analyzing financial documents, and navigating intricate legal frameworks. Honestly, the highlight of many workdays is…lunch. (But with smaller portions, of course!)

But on a good day, you get to see justice done. And on a really good day, you get to be an integral part of it. That's why I wanted to be an attorney as an eight-year-old boy. That's why I enjoy practicing as an attorney today. I like the mental challenge of tackling a problem, finding a solution, and then using that new knowledge for the greater good.

I like to see wrongs made right. I like to see fairness prevail. I like to see the little guy win.

It's an honor and a privilege when my phone rings. For me, it's just a normal day at the office. But for the person on the other end of that line, it is most likely one of the worst days of their life. For them, it's a day that potentially will lead to sleepless nights, nightmares, and endless stress. Being that trusted person that people reach out to is something I never take for granted.

Teddy Roosevelt's "The Man in the Arena" holds a special place in my heart. He wrote, "It is not the critic who counts; not the man who points out how the strong man stumbles, or where the doer of deeds could have done them better. The credit belongs to the man who is actually in the arena, whose face is marred by dust and sweat and blood; who strives valiantly; who errs, who comes short again and again, because there is no effort without error and shortcoming; but who does actually strive to do the deeds; who knows great enthusiasms, the great devotions; who spends himself in a worthy cause; who at the best knows in the end the triumph of high achievement, and who at the worst, if he fails, at least fails while daring greatly, so that *his place shall never be with those cold and timid souls who neither know victory nor defeat*" (emphasis mine).

No, I'm not Perry Mason. *No one is.* But I do represent something that is often hard to find when you're stuck in the deep, dark valley of life.

Hope.

About John

John Mitchell, an enrolled agent and foreign-licensed attorney, boasts over thirty years' expertise in taxation. His tax journey commenced with the manual preparation of 1989 tax returns during the 1990 filing season. Currently, John is deeply immersed in tax planning, consulting, compliance, and controversy resolution. He adeptly handles intricacies with state tax authorities and the IRS, contributing significantly to examinations, collections, appeals, IRS Chief Counsel matters, and litigation support in the United States Tax Court.

In addition to his professional accomplishments, John is a prolific author and a nationally recognized public speaker on tax matters. His influence extends to television, where he not only serves as a regular on-air contributor but also hosts a talk show, establishing himself as a trusted expert in the field. Impressively, John is fluent in Spanish, reaching a native-speaker level of proficiency, a skill honed during his fourteen-year residency in Guadalajara, Mexico.

John's altruistic inclinations are evident in his commitment to justice and advocacy. His fluency in Spanish aids him in connecting with diverse populations, aligning with the principles of social justice advocacy. Furthermore, his extensive experience positions him to support vulnerable populations, utilizing his skills to assist individuals facing tax-related challenges and contributing to societal welfare.

John's dedication to ethical responsibilities is palpable in his role. Navigating the complexities of tax law and compliance demands a steadfast commitment to upholding the rule of law and ensuring fairness. His work underscores his dedication to ethical conduct within the legal profession.

He is a member of the National Association of Enrolled Agents (NAEA), the National Association of Tax Professionals (NATP), the American Bar Association (ABA) Tax Section, and the Texas Society of Enrolled Agents (TXSEA), where he serves on the board of directors.

His community involvement includes volunteering with a local school district to serve as a mentor for underprivileged students and working as a community advisory board member. John also has worked on hundreds of immigration cases as well as volunteering as a tax preparer in support of our military service members and first responders.

On a personal level, John is not just a professional but a devoted family man. His roles as a husband, father, stepfather, and grandfather illuminate the diverse facets of his life. During his downtime, he indulges in leisure pursuits such as being a licensed student pilot and an amateur musician, and enjoying music, books, movies, and quality time with family.

CHAPTER 23

THE MINDSET OF FELLOWSHIP

By Dave DePue

"Jonathan made a covenant with David."
—1 SAMUEL 18:3, HCSB

As a teen, Sam Brownback accelerated into the fast lane as a high school student in the 1970s. Driven by purpose, his rise to greatness continues through his relationships.

Young Sam radiated with an air of destiny. His passion for involvement seemed to engulf all his waking hours. During his high school years, he drove back and forth across Miami County, Kansas, working on Future Farmers of America (FFA) club projects, making friends, and campaigning for election to leadership positions in the youth organization. Soon Sam was crisscrossing the state of Kansas, running for statewide office positions in that organization. Over those years, he wore out the family farm pickup truck, a stick shift, three-on-the-tree Ford F-100.

By twenty-one, Sam had been elected president of Kansas Future Farmers of America and then national vice president of its almost million-member student organization. At Kansas State University, Sam's college classmates rallied to elect him president of the student body.

Sam felt he was ready to apply his learning to a career in the agriculture industry. At graduation, Sam's father, Bob, convinced him that it was not the right time for his son to go into farming. Interest rates were high, and farming bankruptcies were common.

Sam went on to law school. This turned out to be a life-changing move.

A bright young Kansan named Mary Stoffer also went to law school at the University of Kansas. They met and their relationship deepened over the next year. They were married in 1982. Both earned law degrees. Sam joined a small law firm, taught a course on agricultural law at Kansas State University, and was on the radio, broadcasting farm and market news. Mary took a position as clerk for a Kansas Supreme Court Justice, then moved on to work as a trust officer and assistant vice president at a local bank. After the birth of their second child, Mary transitioned to the role of counsel to her ambitious husband and to their growing family. She became the center of gravity for them. Mary's wit and fortitude continue to drive Sam in his rise to greatness.

It was no surprise to Kansas colleagues when Sam was appointed Kansas secretary of agriculture before he was thirty, then the youngest cabinet secretary in the nation. I met Secretary Sam when he offered to help me with some community forums. The mission was to create a seamless educational system for students as they transition among high school, college, and career. Secretary Sam also helped me move these initiatives through the Kansas Legislature. That purpose-driven education system thrives today as the spearhead of our Kansas economic engine.

Are you familiar with the Promise Keepers movement? Sam and I started a Promise Keepers Accountability Group in 1988. We began meeting at 7 a.m. Fridays for coffee at a McDonald's restaurant on Kansas Avenue, a short walk between our office buildings. This quickly grew to four when retired businessman Dean Rabe and Ted Bryan, a retired railroad executive, joined us. Some of our small-group discussions were about our concern for the next generation of state and national leaders. Sam felt we should start by encouraging college students, teenagers who were already stepping into leadership positions.

Driven by a passion to inspire others, Sam gathered up a posse of a dozen friends from across the state. Friends Doug Hinkel and

Dick Coe traveled in from as far away as Wichita and Garden City. Congressman Jim Slattery and his wife, Linda, joined us. We brought in the sponsorship of Topeka Fellowship, an organization in which Sam and I were officers. Topeka Fellowship is the group of friends that manage the Kansas Prayer Breakfast, an annual event patterned after the National Prayer Breakfast. President Eisenhower and US Sen. Frank Carlson of Kansas created the Washington, DC, event to bring national and international leaders together in fellowship.

Our posse set up a steering committee to create and manage programs. Our vibrant meetings were nourished and took root in the crowded parlor of Ted and Ermilou Bryan. The Bryans wanted Becky, their college-aged daughter, to grab a larger vision for life. Sam unveiled a vision for an interactive program called Faith and Values in Leadership.

One hundred fifty emerging student leaders from Kansas colleges and universities were brought into the program each year. I would call each of the college presidents, asking them to nominate and sponsor four student leaders. These students were then invited on the governor's letterhead. The weekend program featured brief presentations from dynamic leaders in various professions, fortified with small-group interaction, mixed with service activities, and joining in with the nearly one thousand dignitaries participating in the annual Kansas Prayer Breakfast.

Two in the first group of students who participated were Tracey Mann and Audrey Haynes. They later served on our steering committee, became dear friends, and married after college. Tracy and Audrey built a successful commercial real estate business together and continued to be immersed in the student leadership program for a dozen years. Tracy was appointed lieutenant governor of Kansas to fill a vacancy in 2018. He was elected in 2020 to serve in the US Congress, representing the people of Kansas in the First District. A couple thousand of our student leadership program "graduates" now serve in significant positions in our communities, in our State, and in national organizations.

The 1990 Kansas elections brought a change of administration, resulting in new cabinet appointments. Sam was succeeded by a secretary of agriculture aligned with the winning party. Sam looked for an open door of opportunity.

Like a thunderclap, that opening came when our friend Jim Slattery called Sam and shared that he would not be running for reelection to Congress. Sam dove into action! He rounded up hundreds of friends, colleagues, and neighbors to sign a petition for the name Sam Brownback to be listed on the ballot. This spirited election campaign won Sam the privilege of representing the people of Kansas in Congress.

"On fire" was the term used to describe the 1994 freshman class in Congress! Half of the members had never held elected office. Many had run under the slogan "Contract for America." Sam helped form a group of forty calling themselves the New Federalists. Sam felt like he was playing in the national football championship and was just handed the ball! This team spearheaded the drive to pass nine of ten Contract bills through the House. The senior senator from Kansas, Bob Dole, mentioned to Sam that he would like to see some of those fiery House members run for Senate.

Skin cancer (melanoma) drove Sam through a period of reflection during the winter of 1995. He saw the personal and social impacts of his race for success. Sam felt that the close relationship with his wife and their three grade school children had suffered. Back in Washington, Sam occupied his evenings in God's Word and in prayer, getting his vertical relationship secure. He came to be at peace by putting God first, his horizontal relationships second, and his work third.

To the surprise of many, our US senator, Bob Dole, resigned to run for the presidency in 1996. Sam rallied his growing team of friends and filed to run for the Senate. His thousands of friends and volunteer workers won the Senate race by a double-digit margin.

Havoc ruled and reigned throughout much of the world

during the 1990s. Senator Sam served on the Foreign Relations Committee for much of his sixteen years in Congress. A spiritual initiative blossomed with the leadership of Rep. Frank Wolf and Sen. Joseph Lieberman. Sam joined them as one of the cosigners of the International Religious Freedom Act, signed into law by President Bill Clinton in 1998. This provided for an international ambassador, who works under the US Department of State. The mission is to recognize nations allowing freedom of expression and to sanction leadership of those countries that repress freedom of conscience.

Sam was completing his second self-limiting term in the US Senate, and there was an open governor's race in Kansas. Friend David Kensinger stepped in to manage the new campaign. Thousands rallied to put Governor Sam in office. Perhaps the next greatest relationship challenge was in finding the talent to quickly fill hundreds of senior-level positions. Governor Sam called on friends from across the state and nation.

In 2018, President Donald Trump appointed Sam as International Ambassador for Religious Freedom. This came twenty years after Sam and congressional friends led the effort to create the office. He was the fifth in a series of International Ambassadors. One staff member of the agency was overheard saying, "They finally appointed someone who is qualified for the job."

Daunting was the mission of the International Ambassador for Religious Freedom. A global challenge indeed. Ambassador Sam represented billions of people impacted by laws and practices that greatly restrict freedom of religion. Sam began to capitalize on the relationships developed during his time serving in Congress and as Kansas governor. He called on leaders in other nations to come alongside and help.

Ambassador Sam and his agency staff quickly planned and organized the first-ever world Ministerial to Advance Religious Freedom. This event was held July 24–26, 2018, in Washington. US Secretary of State Mike Pompeo showed the commitment of the Trump administration by hosting the event.

An alliance of nations was one of Ambassador Sam's first bold initiatives. He sought out leaders of nations who were supportive of religious freedom. Soon this alliance grew to over thirty member nations. This group of ambassadors and national representatives often met monthly, either in person or on conference calls or Zoom meetings. The plan was to host periodic Ministerials (conferences) in a variety of locations where attention to abuse needed to be showcased.

Diplomatic negotiations require many inputs to bring about breakthroughs that help the distressed people. Peer pressure was one of the keys. Notable results included the Abraham Accords, a 2020 peace declaration the United Arab Emirates signed with Israel. A major outcome was the removal of blasphemy laws by the Muslim government of Sudan. These were historic! Ambassador Sam strongly encouraged Middle Eastern leaders, some by personal calls, asking them to release political and religious prisoners during the COVID-19 pandemic. Over two thousand were released at first, and a hundred thousand were set free over the year! Sam's friend fellow Kansan and Secretary of State Pompeo fortified these humanitarian initiatives with economic incentives.

There is no stopping God in the work. The surprise outcome of the 2020 elections kicked off a change of administrations in Washington. January 20, 2021, was inauguration day for US president Joe Biden. This was also the day designated for resignations of executive officers of the previous administration. Ambassador Sam was free of statutory limitations in the mission of protecting freedom of religion. He now was free to include the United States as a focus in the work.

Sam, then as an honorary ambassador, quickly called on a multitude of friends to continue the series of summits and ministerial events. Sam rallied a group of dignitaries and stakeholders to form the National Committee for Religious Freedom. Many virtual meetings later, they set the dates of July 13–15 for the 2021 Summit on Religious Freedom.

The 2021 Summit was organized by citizen Sam and Katrina

Lantos Swett, former chair of the US Commission on Religious Freedom under President Obama. Honorary chairs included members of Congress representing both political parties. Funding support came from friendly organizations, foundations, and individuals. Over seventy cosponsors and supporters included such diverse groups as the National Council of Churches and the All Dulles Area Muslim Society. There was a full house at the Washington, DC, event. Twelve hundred people representing six hundred countries heard the eighty speakers address efforts to protect the endowed rights of humans. Sam concluded: "The religious freedom movement globally catapulted forward."

An example of one of the regional events in the series of Religious Freedom Ministerials is the one held in Prague at the end of November 2023. Sixty countries participated. Sam's Alliance of Nations has become an international movement. All this with a staff of two and an uncountable host of volunteers and sponsors.

———•———

Remember, life moves at the speed of your relationships! Relationships move people and initiatives.

Governor Sam addressed dignitaries at a 2016 Kansas State of the State ceremony: "Look to the person on your right and on your left! Work on getting to know them. This will have a greater impact than many of the policies being addressed in these offices and chambers."

As I close this chapter, here are some tips to remember:

Be interested in the people around you. Be aware of their struggles and celebrations.

Sam would drop personal notes or make calls to show concern or congratulate people who served with him. As chaplain, I accompanied him on numerous hospital visits, to funeral services, and at special recognitions.

Sam and Mary have annual cookouts and celebrations for staff, including former workers.

Sam coordinates an annual spiritual retreat with longtime friends whom he has kept in touch with over the years.

Sam takes a friend or two with him on short trips, sometimes on national and international travel. He rarely goes to lunch alone.

Nearly every day, Sam calls several friends from around the nation and over much of the world. They keep in touch as they work on projects, initiatives, or an upcoming meeting.

Relationship building is the first of a series of principles I encourage in leadership development. Practicing this new habit should bring you almost immediate results in your rise to greatness!

About Dave

Dave DePue is investing a lifetime encouraging young men and women in their rise to greatness. He earned a PhD from The Ohio State University, had an illustrious career in industry, taught in higher education, and served in the Kansas State Capitol for thirty years, the last dozen as a volunteer chaplain.

As a technician, Dave worked in Lockheed's Skunk Works Division. He was on the team building and flight-testing the top-secret SR71 Blackbird Spy Plane. Thirty-two were built. Dave was recognized for team leadership, restoring a fire-damaged Blackbird, saving millions of dollars in a modification program.

As a professor and administrator, Dave led teams to develop statewide undergraduate and graduate education programs that transform students into champions where they live and work.

As a state agency administrator, Dave empowered others to innovate and make breakthroughs in the creation of opportunities for workers and learners of any age. Seamless education and training programs continue fortifying those who are gaining skills and developing their talents.

As Capitol chaplain, Dave encourages leaders in their quest to shape their legacy and become great.

Dave is the author of *Rising to Greatness*—this will be your express lane to success. It's expected to be published in fall 2024. The book's first chapter reveals how the practice of fellowship should bring you almost immediate results in your rise to greatness. Dave was a participant in much of Ambassador Sam Brownback's practice of fellowship in his rise to greatness. The book chronicles how dozens of leaders practiced several key principles and became great. Follow us at www.rising2greatness.com.